rock
& the
CHURCH

by

Bob Larson

CREATION HOUSE
CAROL STREAM, ILLINOIS

FIRST EDITION

Library of Congress Catalog Card Number: 76-158992

CONTENTS

Foreword   5
About the Author   7

Go Ye Into All the World and Groove?   9
High-Powered Put On   15
Uncertain Sounds   29
Whose Is the Winning Play?   39
The Filth and the Fury   53
By Their Fruits   75
Shedding the Myths   83

Footnotes   89

FOREWORD

I am always thrilled to hear of people whose lives have been changed since they met the Savior. In Bob Larson's book *Rock & the Church* we have the evidence of the changed life of the author, and we see a real concern for others based on his personal experiences.

By the age of fifteen, Bob was a disc jockey, had his own band, wrote music, and was caught up in rock and roll. He knows its effect on people; he knows its relationship to the drug scene, and to immorality—and is especially concerned with its impact in Christian circles. Having featured Bob in Word of Life Youth Rallies, we know that he relates positively to young people.

The book is equally good for Christians and non-Christians, but his expose of Christian Rock will jolt a lot of people off their church pews. He pulls no punches when he says there is no place for "Gospel rock" nor for clever entertainers to "sneak Jesus in." The criticism is constructive and shows a sincere love for people and an understanding of their needs.

Bob seems especially sensitive to the danger of the "middle of the road" approach to rock music and of Christians who are trying to relate to the world on its level. Readers will be encouraged to take an objective look at themselves and challenged to act upon what they see.

Jack Wrytzen
Word of Life Fellowship, Inc.
Schroon Lake, N.Y.

5

ABOUT THE AUTHOR

Few observers of that curiosity called "Christian rock" are as qualified as Bob Larson to evaluate its effect on America's churches. Converted as a young man while deeply involved in the rock scene as guitarist and composer, he has since awakened many an adult who should have seen long ago the moral skids that rock music is providing for American youth.

The son of a minister, Bob Larson is now an evangelist, but he was only thirteen when his first popular hit tune was published. At fifteen he had his own rock and roll band and four years later had performed on radio and television shows and entertained capacity audiences in Convention Hall, Atlantic City. While continuing to entertain in personal appearances, he also worked as a radio announcer and disc-jockey. And, in addition he kept on writing music. Recording contracts offers were numerous.

Several scholarships made it possible for Bob to enroll in the pre-med course of a large midwestern university. It was here in March 1963 that his life was changed through meeting T. Texas Tyler, veteran entertainer in country and western music. Tyler introduced Bob to Jesus Christ the Son of God. That spring Bob started on the path of a disciple in total surrender to the Savior.

Through the ministry of David Wilkerson, director and founder of Teen Challenge and author of *The Cross and the Switchblade,* Bob was persuaded to enter Christian service. In 1964 he abandoned the medical profession to enter the ministry. Since then he has lectured at Christian and secular schools, colleges and civic organizations in addition to his schedule of evangelistic crusades. He addressed the student bodies of the foremost Bible colleges of America and has ministered at the request of nearly a dozen evangelical denominations.

The author is currently booked heavily as a lecturer in public schools where he presents a moral analysis of rock music. Through this outreach alone he speaks to more than half a million students in more than five hundred high schools and colleges each year.

Bob Larson knows his subject firsthand. He writes with the clarity and strength of someone talking about a subject he understands. He enjoys the distinction of being one of the finest recording guitarists today, in addition to his versatile talents as a composer, singer, author, lecturer and evangelist.

His first book, *Rock and Roll: The Devil's Diversion,* has had several printings and has already had profound influence upon the lives of thousands of teenagers the world over.

The Publishers

chapter one

GO YE

INTO ALL THE WORLD

AND GROOVE?

Strange music is being heard across the broad expanse of our country today. Its lyrics are sprinkled heavily with words from the Bible; its singers croon, as if seeking earnestly a filling of the Spirit; albums featuring "Jesus rock" are finding their way into the homes of true believers.

Is it all the harbinger of a fantastic spiritual revival? Unfortunately, such is hardly the case, as this behind-the-scenes documentary volume will reveal. Rock music is creating a crisis in the church. As in every moral crisis, God's people are forced to take a stand against that which is evil.

If you have pretended to see the Gospel of Jesus Christ in these bizarre songs this book will leave you disillusioned and informed.

Teenagers often write expressing their thanks and encouragement for a voice in the wilderness against rock and roll. Some, however, write to condemn my stand. Each week the mail brings dozens of letters from interested readers. Increasingly my correspondents want more detailed information, asking: "What is your opinion of Christian rock music?"

The following letter, written by a student in Bible college, sums up the searching of many:

> I read your book *Rock & Roll: The Devil's Diversion* and enjoyed it very much. It answered many of my questions about rock. I was saved not long ago and have been attending Bible school ever since. God has called me to work among youth to win them to Christ. I have one question yet in my mind. Can a person play rock music with a beat and really be effective for Christ? I wonder if the sound is of the flesh or not. I know that there is no true Christian "anointing" in the music yet the words sometimes have a message. I know others use this medium to reach youth but do they get a cheap conversion because of the compromise? Do they think because they were won under this type of music that rock isn't wrong? I'll be going into full-time Christian work this summer and I don't want to be deceiving kids by compromise. Do youth actually look up to a Christian who uses this type of music as a spiritual leader or as just another entertainer? Can I really be an effective spiritual leader and use this music and afterwards preach to them?

Although some people are able to defend "Christian rock," the majority of correspondents express sincere perplexity about what their stand should be. Those who question the validity of Christian rock do not want to judge wrongly people who are seeking to use the medium as a true witness for Christ. But they cannot accept the premise that rock is *the* medium to reach the "now" generation for God. This confusion is found among adults and teens alike. They want to know if the issues are black and white or if perhaps there are some gray shades that require a specialized approach in communicating the Gospel.

One thing is certain: God is not the author of confusion. Belief in this scriptural premise leads to the conclusion that the Christian rock crisis is not of God, for divisiveness cannot bring glory to God. In most arguments there are two sides, but that rule cannot apply to a situation where Christian principles are disputed. In such instances there is only one position that is scripturally supportable.

The purpose of this book is not to raise more indecision or merely to voice another personal opinion on an already controversial issue. It is written rather with a prayer that it will resolve the Christian rock crisis in a manner consistent with evangelical theological convictions through the help of the Holy Spirit.

I am amazed that the evangelical church should hesitate for a moment in rejecting rock as an evangelistic medium. I vividly recall the early days when even secular people denounced the eroticism of rock. When Elvis Presley first appeared on the Ed Sullivan show he was shot only from his waist up. Communist countries quickly forbade the new fad called rock and roll. And a senate investigating committee was formed to explore its relationship to juvenile delinquency that was continuing to rise.

But rock has outlasted the fad stage. Public attitude has benignly accepted it—even endorsed it. This shift in attitude could logically be expected from an unregenerate world. But the Christian rock crisis has resulted from a loose attitude toward rock on the part of the evangelical church. Today it is not only tolerated but often accepted in the church program as part of its ministry to young members and as part of its evangelistic outreach.

11

I recall visiting a reptile garden some years back with a knowledgeable guide. The subject of new employees came up. I inquired whether the veteran snake handlers had to watch the newcomers closely so they would not be bitten.

"No," came the suprising answer. "At first an employee has no problem. He is constantly aware of the danger. The real trouble comes later after he has been around the snakes so long without being bitten that he grows careless—then he runs a great risk of being struck."

A decade and a half ago the venom of rock music frightened decent people in the world. Today, it engenders an attitude of apathy and indifference—even in the church!

One might have anticipated the acceptance of rock in liberal churches as inevitable with their strong emphasis on social service rather than biblical ministry. Modernistic churches have a history of compromise in conforming to the standards of the world. Their liberal members are being led, rather than providing leadership. When rock music came into vogue it was quickly accepted by many liberal churches. But the disturbing fact is: "Christian rock" evangelism is far more prevalent today in evangelical congregations than in liberal churches. The avant garde in Christian rock can be found almost exclusively among those who supposedly profess a personal relationship with Christ. Many evangelical church leaders, consciously or unconsciously, have turned to rock music as their major thrust in youth evangelism.

I first became aware of the Christian rock crisis in the fall of 1969. At that time it was my privilege to address the annual American ·Association of Bible Colleges and the National Church Music Fellowship Convention in Chicago. At these sessions I had the opportunity to talk to scores of evangelical church leaders from all parts of America. Previously I had heard of instances of Christian rock in evangelical circles, but my position against it kept me from being invited to such a church. So I had few direct confrontations with it.

I'll admit, I was a bit unsuspecting about rock invading the church. My former familiarity with rock music as an unconverted rock guitarist, composer, and singer made the compound adjective "Christian rock" sound incongruous.

The convention for church musicians was eye-opening. Again and again I heard dedicated men express concern that rock music was becoming entrenched in the evangelical church despite their opposition.

In 1970 "Christian rock" captivated the religious youth scene. What had previously been a mere rumble now fell like a thunder clap on the church. Unprincipled laymen, mistaken pastors and unconsecrated teenagers were all caught in its onslaught. Christian rock, once a mere ripple on the surface became a tidal wave that swept unsuspecting churches into a totally new emphasis in evangelistic priorities. Since that Chicago meeting in 1969 my naivete has been replaced by shock, prayerful concern, and a determination to speak forcefully and clearly on this issue.

History has recorded church music crises in the past, but Christian rock is a totally new problem. The Reformation, for example had a profound effect upon the musical idioms of the church. Prior to the sixteenth century, church music was limited to complex choir arrangements. Well-disciplined singers often made church music more of an aesthetic production than a medium to communicate the Gospel.

Luther and Calvin both sought to introduce simple melodies and lyrics that more closely resembled the

13

vernacular of the laity. Lovers of tradition in the Catholic church resented this approach. They feared and attacked the musical trends brought about by the awakening that stirred the people of God. But one point must be emphasized: The musical innovators of the sixteenth century always expressed a firm scriptural commitment in the adoption of new methods. They stressed a cautious attitude in their endeavors.

How unlike the present Christian rock enthusiasts! They defend their policies by arguing from the pragmatic viewpoint. "It brings in the kids and makes the church relevant," they say.

Church music should contribute to worship and evangelism. In doing so it ought to support and promote biblical theology. Christian rock does neither. The present crisis is therefore more than a dispute regarding the proper choice of musical idiom. It is a controversy that is essentially theological in nature. I am convinced that Satan has chosen the field of church music as a battleground to launch an attack. As a result, this generation of believers is caught in a fierce spiritual struggle.

With this viewpoint, let us take a closer look at the inroads of Christian rock within the church.

chapter two

HIGH-POWERED

PUT ON

"Spirit in the Sky"—the title of a gospel song? Hardly! This song was number one on the rock charts in the spring of 1970 and its popularity caused many Christian teenagers to rejoice. They naively concluded that at last, according to their suppositions, a "Christian" song had topped the hit list.

Nothing could be more wrong, yet one point is significant: Rock in more recent months has been enamored with religious themes. From a superficial standpoint, the message of such songs appears to be sympathetic toward the Christian faith. Many Christian rock enthusiasts eagerly applauded the "spiritual revival" in hit tunes. But such conclusions were unfounded. Their hope that the Holy Spirit was moving afresh in the pop tunes of the day was little more than wishful thinking.

Actually, religion in rock lyrics is not new but rock tunes in the past treated Christianity with contempt. Most of them were sung by hostile and blasphemous entertainers with no regard for the Almighty. Three prominent songs in 1965 featured Christian themes. One titled "Sinner Man" glorified a promiscuous life style and "The Seventh Son" contained a reference to demonism and spoke of healing the sick and raising the dead.

The Byrds recorded the other, "Turn, Turn, Turn," a pacifist song which recited the words to the third chapter of Ecclesiastes over the background of folk-rock music.

In 1967 Neil Diamond wrote and recorded a million-seller titled "I Thank the Lord." The lyrics were not an expression of appreciation toward God but only a glib and casual use of the word "Lord."

The 1968 Grammy award-winning song was "Mrs. Robinson." Recorded and written by Simon and Garfunkel, the words ridiculed the existence of heaven and the person of Christ.

One of the top tunes in early 1969 was recorded by Arthur Brown, a performer who has dedicated his life to ridiculing religious themes. His song, "Fire," began with a mockery of hell as Mr. Brown lyrically personified himself as the god of hellfire.

Later in 1969 Joe South wrote and recorded, "Games People Play." It carried a line that was an obvious derision of street witnessing.

In a similar vein at about the same time, Neil Diamond wrote and recorded a song contemptuous of a tent evangelist: "Brother Love's Traveling Salvation Show." *Hit Parader* magazine quoted Diamond's admission that his song was done as a putdown of revival meetings.[1]

Also in 1969 an example of sacrilege in rock was the top-selling tune "In the Year 2525." The lyrics featured a pessimistic view of life in the future with apparent disdain for belief in the Second Coming of Christ. That same year even the Cowsills got into the act with a song called, "The Prophecy of Daniel & John the Divine." Written about the Anti-Christ, the refrain

16

referred to his number "six, six, six." Nilsson ended the year with a typical rock spoof critical of Christianity, "I Guess the Lord Must be in New York City,"

The jazz-rock group Blood, Sweat & Tears has been particularly curious about religion. They have offered many songs on the subject of which the following three are examples: 1) "And When I Die"—the lyrics mention demons while swearing there is no heaven and praying there is no hell; 2) "Hi-De-Ho"—the singer in this tune speaks of a confrontation with the devil that draws similarities with the temptation of Christ in the wilderness; 3) "Lucretia Mac Evil"—the story in song is that of a prostitute whose soul has been sold to the devil on the day she was born.

The Rolling Stones produced an album in 1968 titled, "Their Satanic Majesty's Request." (How appropriate!) On their album "Beggers Banquet" they recorded two songs in the religious category. The first was titled "Sympathy for the Devil" and included a glorification of none other than satan. The second song is "Prodigal Son." Its lyrics indicate that with respect to the personal life style of the Stones they were apt performers for such a song.

The most dramatic mockery of Christ has been the rock opera "Tommy," as performed by The Who. In 1970 alone the album earned well in excess of five million dollars! The extravaganza, performed at the Metropolitan Opera House, is a parable about a boy who grows deaf, dumb, and blind after watching his father kill his mother's lover. Later he is miraculously cured and becomes a pinball champion and messiah and finally the leader of a quasi-religious state. The production is a metaphoric mockery of Jesus Christ, the Son of God. It contains one song that vividly describes a child molestation scene ("Fiddle, Uncle Ernie, Fiddle").[2]

Broadway has not overlooked the rock religious act. The musical "Salvation" takes up where "Hair" left off.

The latest and most disturbing scene in the blasphemy of rock is called "Satan Rock," performed by groups such as The Damnation of Adam Blessing, Coven, and Black Sabbath. Coven is promoted by lines such as "Coven destroys minds and reaps souls." Black Sabbath was introduced to the British press by a party featuring the mock sword sacrifice of a semi-nude girl. The Damnation of Adam Blessing is described as a "satanic happening etched on lacquer." The trend is not a put-on. Many hippie communities now practice occultism to the accompaniment of their own special rock musical liturgy.

Against the background of popular rock songs that are openly sacrilegious has sprung up a new trend toward "Jesus Rock." These songs give the impression that Christ has at last gained wide acceptance. The anti-scriptural overtones are muted and obscured so that the uncritical listener can be deceived into thinking that rock has changed its ways.

Rolling Stone, the major underground rock magazine, assessed the situation by saying, "Jesus rock is just about the hottest thing going these days."[3] *Billboard,* the foremost periodical in the record industry, suggested: "Many of the major rock groups are deep into the religious groove." [4]

It's logical for the secular world to swallow religion in rock because it has little knowledge of Scripture and no discernment. But Christian people have no such excuse. I have been profoundly disturbed by the fact that many believers have been duped into believing that God, rather than satan, is behind the thrust of Jesus rock. Let us look more closely at the developing trends of supposedly pro-religious themes in rock and determine their scriptural validity.

18

The number which triggered the avalanche of Jesus rock tunes was the 1969 hit, "Oh, Happy Day," that rose to the spot of the number five single in the nation. A white audience somewhat unfamiliar with black gospel music was captivated by its rock beat and rhythm and blues arrangement. With a hit tune on their hands the Edwin Hawkins singers launched upon an extensive nightclub tour.

While there is nothing unscriptural in the lyrics of "Oh, Happy Day" most groups performing the song live have overdone its soul-rock beat. The final four bars of the song are usually repeated over and over— not to re-emphasize the message, but to whip listeners into the frenzy that accompanies rock.

Hard on the heels of "Oh, Happy Day" came Lawrence Reynolds' big hit in the fall of 1969, "Jesus Is a Soul Man." My first exposure to this song came when I read a *Billboard* advertisement concerning its release. A group of hippies were pictured sitting in the woods drinking wine. The caption read, " 'Jesus Is a Soul Man,' a single to celebrate." My first reaction was, "Who are they trying to put on?"

A few days later some Christian teenagers asked me enthusiastically if I had heard the "wonderful new Christian song on the top-forty, 'Jesus Is a Soul Man.'" I could hardly believe that Christian teenagers could be that deceived by the "super-hippie" image of Christ. Jesus is called many things in the Bible (e.g., "The Lamb of God," "The Prince of Peace," "The King of Kings," "Lord of Lords," "The Mighty God," etc.) but never a "Soul Man." The term "soul" does not refer to that eternal entity that shall live after death. It's an adjective borrowed from the black community referring to a life style separated from the worship of the divine Savior. The song emphasizes the humanity of Jesus, playing down His incarnation. The song brings Christ to the level of man without acknowledging that He is God who can lift men from their sin unto righteousness. The Lordship of Christ is nowhere expressed in the song. Instead, the lyrics focus on the word "soul" that is often attached with vulgar associations.

I am reminded of a comment by Arthur Brown, who was mentioned earlier in the chapter. He explained, "Soul....is sex!" [5]

On the backliner of this song's album jacket the story of how "Jesus Is a Soul Man" came to be written is told. Obviously, Lawrence Reynolds had only secular, commercial concerns on his mind. He was attempting to catch the coattails of the popular song, "Oh, Happy Day" and Jesus rock.

If you still think the song was written to glorify Christ, check the flip side of the single, "Jesus Is a Soul Man." Also written and recorded by Mr. Reynolds, it is entitled: "I Know a Good Girl When I Hold One." The song is not the kind that emanates from a life of deep, spiritual commitment and discernment!

In the wake of "Soul Man" came dozens of others attempting to ride the "Jesus rock" bandwagon. The Byrds recorded "Jesus Is Just All Right," although they never got around to saying why. The Jefferson Airplane recorded a subtle mockery titled, "Good Shepherd." A lesser known underground rock group called Aum released an album they titled, "Ressurrection." On the album's jacket the leader of Aum is depicted as Jesus Christ. Along with "Resurrection" in this album is another called, "God Is Back In Town."

Bob Dylan's album "New Morning" contained two songs with religious themes, "Father of Night" and "Three Angels"—quite a switch from his earlier songs of drugs and protest. James Taylor in his lament, "Fire and Rain" began the second verse with "Look down

20

upon me, Jesus." His follow-up hit "Country Road" again alluded to Christ with the line "sail on home to Jesus."

An ensemble called The Band on its Capitol LP "Stage Fright" have a cut called, "Daniel and the Sacred Harp." Both the Beatles' single "Let It Be" and Simon and Garfunkel's "Bridge Over Troubled Waters" featured a gospel style piano sounding as though it came right out of a revival meeting. The former makes the point of guidance beyond human wisdom which the singer receives in "times of trouble" when "Mother Mary comes to me."

Have the Beatles at last turned to Christianity? Hardly. All four had been practicing Hindus under the guise of transcendental meditation described fully in the author's book *Hippies, Hindus, and Rock & Roll* and have never recanted on that commitment. John Lemmon has publicly stated that "Let It Be" was written about Paul McCartney's mother, named Mary.

Without exception, the personal lives of the secular rock musicians recording Jesus rock directly contradict the supposed "Christian" message their songs convey. Obviously, their only interest is in capitalizing on a fad. This fact was most evident in early 1971 when folk singer Judy Collins recorded an acappela version of the beloved hymn "Amazing Grace." This rendition actually made it into the "top ten" on the rock charts. At the time, Miss Collins (at one time an identified communist) was pregnant with child by a man she publicly proclaimed as having no intentions of marrying!

Many singers and musicians whose background has been solely in gospel music have joined the Jesus rock performers. Organist Billy Preston recorded a single for the Beatles' Apple label which was called, "That's the Way God Planned It." Mylon LeFevre, formerly of

21

the LeFevres gospel group, is attempting to carve out a niche with gospel rock on Cotillion Records. Shelby Singleton, president of Plantation Records, is going all out on Jesus rock with a full-scale production lineup including a record recently released by Dee Mullins called, "Remember Bethlehem." Its lyrics describe the birth of Jesus to the beat of rock. Singleton also issued an album of Jesus rock featuring the U. S. Apple Corps. Bergen White also has a record called "Spread the Word" and a single by the Sweet Revival titled, "Will the Real Jesus Please Stand Up."

Singleton is convinced that the religious interest of rock is not a fad. "I think Jesus rock is a trend," he said. "Too many records are happening to be accidental." [6]

The short-lived rock "super-group" called Blind Faith joined the trend. On their only album they recorded an Eric Clapton song, "In the Presence of the Lord." Dozens of Christian teenagers have tried to convince me that this song is an expression of a true Christian believer. That's a little hard to swallow, however, since Clapton has been busted for drug possession and at no time has declared himself to be a born-again Christian.

In a recent interview by the editors of a well-known rock magazine Clapton sprinkled his comments with profanity and admitted his surprise at people trying to corollate "In the Presence of the Lord" with the Bible. [7] The song is, in fact, sacrilegious because the hypocritical Eric Clapton sings a pretense of praising Christ when in reality he does not serve Him. This is underscored by the fact that the album jacket was sold with an alternate cover picture. One was a campy picture of the group with their musical instruments. The alternate, which was sold under the counter, featured a front view of a young teenage girl completely nude. *This album jacket received a Grammy Award nomination!*

The Jesus rock phenomenon peaked in the spring of 1970 when "Spirit in the Sky" reached the top spot across the nation. Soon after its release I was lecturing at an evangelical Bible seminary. After my anti-rock presentation the student body president vehemently opposed my views. During the course of our conversation he asked if I had heard the new release, "Spirit in the Sky."

I had not.

He went on to declare that this song expressed firm faith in Jesus Christ. He was not alone. Christian teens by the dozens soon deluged me with messages defending this song as an example of how at last the world was waking up to the reality of Jesus.

I wonder if those who praise and defend "Spirit in the Sky" have really heard the words—its lyrics are not scriptural. The third verse expresses the thought that the singer has never sinned. This is a contradiction of Romans 3:23, "For all have sinned and come short of the glory of God." The album was advertized by a picture of its writer and singer Norman Greenbaum captioned, "I Am Curious (Greenbaum)"—a reference to the morally repulsive "sex-ploitation" Swedish film, "I Am Curious (Yellow)." In an interview Greenbaum said, "A lot of people looked at 'Spirit in the Sky' as a one-type religion. I see the song as being about simple togetherness." [8]

Greenbaum later revealed his purposes in writing the song. "I wanted to write a thing called a religious song." he said. "Jesus Christ is popular and in actuality I just used the most popular religious character in my song. Some people wrote and thanked me because of my song and are disappointed to find out that I'm not a Christian and I don't go to church." [9] The writer is

Jewish and admits he doesn't believe in the diety of Jesus Christ.

Those who still doubt the intentions of Norman Greenbaum should note that previous to his song "Spirit in the Sky" he wrote and released the song, "The Eggplant that Ate Chicago." Following his "Spirit" song he composed and released "Canned Ham." Do these songs sound as though they were born in the heart of a man with spiritual perception?

The next step taken by Jesus rock was the Pacific Gas and Electric's summer hit, "Are you Ready?" The lyrics ask if the listener is prepared to sit by God's throne. This song too was interpreted as a Christian testimony since one member of the group professed to be a Christian at the time the song was a hit. He has now left the group. For several reasons his testimony seemed questionable. First, Pacific Gas & Electric, as do all rock groups, frequently appears in the pot-intoxicated rock ballrooms that form the rock circuit. They appeared recently with such acts as Country Joe (of F.I.S.H. Cheer fame), and with the cast of "Hair" at a summer Festival for Peace raising money for leftist peace candidates and communist front organizations. One of their albums offers the revolutionary rock MC 5 song "Motor City's Burning." The lyrics advocate a riotous destruction of Detroit, Michigan, with words that would not be repeated even at a stag party. On the jacket's inside cover one member of the band is photographed wearing an American flag desecrated and made into a shirt!

With the rise in popularity of Jesus rock it was inevitable that a creedal statement of faith should emerge. In the fall of 1970 Teegarden & Van Winkle finally presented the "apostle's creed" of the rock generation: "God, Love and Rock & Roll." The lyrics proclaim, "We believe in God, love and rock and roll." Considering that the term "rock and roll" was originally a descriptive sex expression this line might be translated, "We believe in God, love, and promiscuous sexual intercourse." A look at the morality of the rock culture would convince anyone that this creed mirrors what its fans really worship.

New fuel was added to the Jesus rock thrust when in late 1970 Decca records released the soundtrack of the religious rock opera "Jesus Christ—Superstar." Early record sales predicted that it might become the biggest money-making album of all time. The 87-minute, two-LP album pictures Christ as merely a humanitarian radical thinker, who is followed like a rock star. Judas is treated sympathetically as a sincere but coniving manager. Mary Magdalene is the prostitute of Christ's group and an affair between her and Jesus is suggested. Toward the end of the opera Christ is shown drunk with the Apostles at the Last Supper.

In its review *Time* stated that in "Superstar," the crucifixion is seen to be the result of bungling self-indulgence, and Jesus' faith in his divinity and the hope of Resurrection, as delusions." [10]

Tim Rice, the librettist who worked with composer Andrew Webber to produce "Superstar," admitted: "It happens that we don't see Christ as God, but simply the right man at the right time in the right place." [11]

Still there are some evangelical Christians who choose to ignore the blasphemy of "Superstar" in favor of praising it as still another example of the "infiltration of the Gospel into the rock music scene." Ironically, nearly every secular review I have consulted has made special note of the fact that in "Superstar" all references to the resurrection have been obviously, deliberately omitted.

Early in 1971, Jesus rock enthusiasts again thought they had topped the charts when George Harrison's

"My Sweet Lord" became the top song on the rock charts. Background voices (dubbed in by Harrison himself) sang "Hallelujah!" while the lyrics of the song suggested that Harrison really wanted to feel God but "it takes so long."

Harrison, despite his split with Maharishi Mahesh Yogi, still practices transcendental meditation as a firm devotee of Hinduism. The line, "it takes so long," is a reference to the meditative processes of Hinduism and oriental mysticism in which union and communion with God are gradual but never completely achieved. This, of course, is in direct contrast to the evangelical belief of instantaneous conversion and intimate companionship with God through Christ.

In a way, the lyrics are the plaintive cry of one who seeks to know God but can never do so by the heathen route of Hinduism. Harrison really gives himself away in the final refrain in which the background voices switch from "Hallelujahs" to the "Hare Krishna" chant.

The "Lord" referred to throughout the song is not the "Lord Jesus Christ." Hindus refer to their God as "Lord" also. The complete chant goes: *Hare Krishna, Krishna, Krishna, Hare, Hare, Hare Rama, Hare Rama, Rama, Rama, Hare, Hare.*

"Hare" is the name of Vishnu, the Hindu god who offers delightful pleasure. "Rama" is the incarnation of Vishnu. Krishna is the "god-narrator" of the *Bhagavada-Gita*—sacred text of Hinduism.

To faithful Hindus, such as Harrison, the chant is literally the incarnation of the different names, or aspects, of the Hindu god. Since Christians know these gods to be false (in reality, demon spirits), "My Sweet Lord" is actually a prayer of demon possession (a claim substantiated in the author's book, *Hippies, Hindus, and Rock & Roll*).

Imagine such a song, no matter how pretty it may be melodically, becoming the top-selling song in a nation such as America. Even more disturbing is the fact that some Christian teens are duped by it. They defend it as another example of the Holy Spirit at work in Jesus rock music!

Any time the world begins to sing about Jesus, Christians should beware. If it's to his advantage, satan will allow rock to have religious overtones. He would like to give the appearance that the Gospel is being favorably received by the rock music world.

But just because the world is talking and singing about Jesus can be no sign of comfort to true Christians. The world hates Christ as much as it did when the multitudes crucified Him. Don't be gullible! When rock musicians speak and sing of Christ, be on the defensive. What they say might sound good at first but their ultimate aim is probably to discredit the Gospel and the person of Christ. Jesus rock is "another gospel," of which the Apostle Paul warned the Galatians to beware. He adds in the strongest language that those who preach it should be accursed.

I am not alone in rejecting the distortion of Christianity in Jesus rock. The Rev. John Sheerin, editor of *The Catholic World,* said of religious lyrics in modern rock songs: "They give only a misty, shadowy picture of Jesus that has scant resemblance to the Jesus of history and Christian belief. It's in line with the interest in Eastern mysticism current in youth circles today with its appeal mainly in chants and rhythms rather than the specific meanings of the lyrics." Such music offers, in the view of Father Sheerin, "a purely romanticized image of Jesus but fails to face up to the fact of Jesus which is essential to genuine faith."

Those who defend Jesus rock ought to listen to an analysis of rock and religion contained in the underground rock magazine, *Rolling Stone.* In the April 16, 1970 issue a record reviewer said of Jesus rock, "All of it is tongue-in-cheek of course. No one really believes a word of it. As Captain Beefheart shouts out in one of his songs, it's sort of 'Jesus keep on comin'/ Yer the best dressed.'" [12]

From a secular viewpoint, the fusion of rock and religion was inevitable because today's rock is a form of religion. The Woodstocks of today are the revival meetings of the rock generation. Believe it or not, the summer 1970 rock fest in Rotterdam, Holland— that was attended by a hundred thousand young people with long hours of sex, dope and music—was concluded when the Byrds climaxed the affair by singing, "Amazing Grace." [13]

Rock musicians and singers are not only exponents of a musical form. They are secular gods to which young people easily relate because they embody the characteristics of this generation. They advocate promiscuous love, decry war, wear freaky clothing and long hair. Most important of all, they are fiercely anti-establishment.

What other religion of youth could command such a mass of believers (e.g., the half-million gathered at Woodstock) whose life style and social and moral ethic have so much in common? Dr. Barry Ulanov, head of the English Department of Barnard College in New York City, said: "Rock might be a liturgical music for a new kind of religion." [14]

New examples of Jesus rock will keep emerging. This much is certain now: whatever treatment rock may give Christianity, the result will certainly not be scripturally supportable if current trends are any indication. Again I must emphasize that the reader ought to approach cautiously any portrayal by rock groups of Jesus Christ, remember that "the devils also believe, and tremble" (James 2:19).

chapter three

UNCERTAIN

SOUNDS

This is my story, this is my song.
Praising my Savior all the day long.

The comforting strains of "Blessed Assurance" would appear to the average Christian as being totally unsuited to the accompaniment of rock music. Not so to the exploiters. Much to my shock and amazement I heard even this beloved favorite tainted by the crude vibrations of soul rock.

I only wish this were an isolated example of rock's invasion of the church, but it isn't. If time and space permitted, I could fill this book with scores of additional examples.

In New England, a Christian disc jockey produces a weekly two-hour radio show in which he uses rock songs. He also interviews Christian entertainers and adds his own comments about religion. On one occasion this disc jockey cited George Harrison as an example of a popular entertainer who produces songs with a religious message. "George Harrison doesn't have a born-again experience yet, but I believe God has it in His plan for him," he declared. [1]

In another part of the country a professing evangelical youth minister calls himself the "Soul Man" and conducts a weekly rock program on which he plays Christian rock records along with the secular top thirty. [2]

For Easter 1970, an international Christian youth organization promoted a three-day Faith Festival as an "answer" to rock fare. After plenty of Christian rock music (some "answer"!) the final night was concluded with a "brief call to Christ" with approximately five hundred young people making "decisions." [3]

In El Paso, Texas, six hundred young people "made commitments to Christ in one night of old-fashioned revival helped along by the hard rock sound of long-haired Christian musicians." [4]

Many Christian youth organizations, along with prominent Bible college and university leaders, and well-known Christian personalities have joined efforts to promote religion's adaptation to rock. Even the Salvation Army has exchanged its brass band for a rock group called "The Persuaders."

Some of the justification for such an approach involves incredible logic. A record review section in a foremost Christian periodical [5] concluded that a certain Christian rock recording "will be loved or detested —depending on the age, musical background, taste and/or mood of the listener."

The inference drawn is that those who oppose such a record must be over thirty, have no musical background in rock, be culturally turned off by rock by reason of personal taste, and be characterized as an emotionally solemn individual. Since I am exact opposite of all the foregoing descriptions I'd like to know how the reviewer would explain my rejection of that particular rock record.

Another magazine writer promoting Christian rock reviewed a rendition of "Peace in the Valley." He said: "Traditionalists might be a little shaken at first, but even some of them will come around . . . that is, if they can relate to the young at all." [6] The reviewer implies that acceptance of Christian rock is only a matter of time and that those who reject it must have little concern for reaching youth with the Gospel. Still another advocate of Christian rock reasoned: "We are aware that you are troubled by the strange sounds and vibrations that come out of our stereos. To this we say, 'Your music was fine for you in your generation, but the youth of today have their own rhythm and beat.'" [7] Such a conclusion is without historical perspective and is blind to the ability of certain modern rhythms and beats to induce demon influence.

For all their sense of avant garde in the realm of Christian rock, evangelicals are Johnny-come-latelys. The liberal churchmen have beat them to it, as I mentioned in chapter one. In 1967 the Electric Prunes did an album called "Mass in F Minor." In 1969 an underground group, Mind Garage, produced an "Electric Liturgy" which was performed at St. Mark's Cathedral in New York. Duke Ellington, the famous jazz performer, packed the Episcopal Cathedral of Saint John the Divine when he presented a worship service of jazz and dancing.

A rock service at Chicago's Episcopal church featured such songs as Dylan's "The Times They Are A-Changin" which drew capacity crowds.

Four Protestant churches in the vicinity of Warsaw, Indiana, cooperate each summer to provide early morning Sunday services in a tent-like theater-in-the-round. These services vary from jazz to modern dance —even offering the medium of the play.

Not long ago two young rabbis and two laymen presented a multi-media religious service. Their technique was to use two screens, one showing scenes of atrocities from Hitler's Germany, the other showing scenes from the Democratic National Convention in Chicago. Background music was provided by Phil Ochs singing, "Days of Decision."

Harvey Cox, Professor of Divinity at Harvard University, celebrated a liturgy at a Boston discotheque to the accompaniment of a rock band called the Apocrypha. The song was entitled, "I Can't Get No Satisfaction," [8] with lyrics referring to both sexual promiscuity and menstruation!

Despite such a checkered history, evangelical churches have more recently taken the lead in introducing and promoting Christian rock. It started with the influence of folk songs in the late sixties. But today the harmless folk tunes have been replaced in some churches by what can only be described as hard and acid rock. The use of the guitar, bass, drums and other musical instruments is not new to many evangelicals. Such churches have often featured an assortment of instruments accompanying their congregational singing in a subdued manner. But no longer. Even church musicians who have formerly insisted upon classical forms of church music have stood by uncritical. Thus evangelicals sometimes find themselves promoting Christian rock and defending their actions to religious liberals who are opposed to it.

A veteran pianist for a respected evangelist is a promoter of sacred rock while a Roman Catholic journalist denounces Christian rock as music that "lacks not only the devotional quality, but also the particular grace of art because it gives us in the raw those cultural traits that were not influenced by Christian ethics." [9]

My knowledge of Christian rock at this point may seem purely academic or that of one who would have to admit as Will Rogers did: "I only know what I read in the newspapers." However, I have had the opportunity to see many Christian groups engaged in rock music. Three such instances suggest themselves because they represent three basic approaches of Christian rock. In order to keep this book oriented to an indictment of principles rather than of people I shall omit the names of each group discussed.

The three types of approaches are: (1) The "Rock of Ages" approach, (2) The "Get the Message?" approach, and (3) The "Guess Why We're Here!" approach.

The first is characterized by the use of mostly sacred songs done to a rock beat. The group in question was observed presenting an open-air public performance. Several recent pop and rock hits were included in the program but the majority of songs were familiar hymns such as "The Solid Rock," with emphasis upon the "rock." Religious overtones were present, but not until two-thirds of the program had passed did one of the singers give a testimony of conversion to Christ, and that was ambiguous, to say the least. The back-up instruments for the dozen or so singers consisted of the typical rock essentials (drums, bass, guitar, electronic organ) plus a brass section. In spite of the somewhat limited staging area there was plenty of gesticulatory choreography. Obvious restraint was necessary to keep the singers from letting loose a full-fledged frug to "Blessed Assurance." The musicians had a rock field day until they were restrained by the musical arrangement in accompaniment to a patriotic medley. In fact, the patriotic segment was the only portion of the "show" that they had taste enough not to smother with rock.

To their credit only a third of the program was secular rock. The moderator did give a weak invitation at the close, appealing for listeners to give their hearts to Christ. No opportunity was given for them to "come forward" (the environment and logistics would have been a problem), but those desiring Christ were asked to lift hands to indicate they were requesting prayer.

I left the meeting that day feeling that those sincere young people had wasted a lot of effort and musical talent in a superficial approach that could never, never produce substantial spiritual fruit.

The second approach, "Get the message?" is characterized by pop and rock songs designed to compliment the Gospel. This performance took place in a youth chapel immediately following the Sunday evening service in one of America's foremost evangelical churches. The five-member rock group, consisting of Bible college students, was introduced by the youth pastor who emphasized how many years they had been playing together. This, he intimated, was indicative of their spiritual success—a correlation that left me puzzled.

The two attractive female members were appropriately dressed in mini skirts. They used their sex appeal to the best advantage. A "Three Dog Night" number started the program, followed by five more successive hard rock songs that set the mood for the evening. The moderator then explained their purpose by saying, "I suppose you're wondering why we haven't yet said anything about Christ. We're not going to do so tonight because later this week we'll be putting on a concert in the church sanctuary and we invite you back when we'll tell you about our faith in God."

I could only pray that no one in the audience was

destined to be a fatality because of an accident or disease before the next concert when they would allegedly hear this most important message.

Several other secular tunes were introduced by the group's spokesman with the statement, "Listen closely to the message of this song. We hope you understand it." Considering the volume of the drums and lead guitar, their apprehensiveness about the message was understandable. A few Christian rock songs were thrown in with the secular rock hits, but that was not the highlight of the program. That occurred when they emphasized that the audience listen carefully to the words of Bob Dylan's "I Shall Be Released." I did and recognized the tune as the one Dylan had written to extol the virtues of Hinduism and Eastern mysticism. (See the author's book *Hippies, Hindus and Rock and Roll.*)

Not a word of Christian testimony was offered in that program. I was relieved when it was finally over. There had been no invocation so I certainly did not expect a benediction and least of all an invitation. I was right. I left weeping unashamedly, not for the Christian rock group, but for the unsaved teenagers hopelessly searching for the water of life. I knew many of them might never again have the opportunity to receive Christ.

The third and last approach, "Guess Why We're Here!" offers a secular program designed to make the listeners guess, "Why do you think we're doing this for free?"

While visiting one of Southern California's major tourist centers, I passed by the entertainment grandstand and overheard the sounds of a fully-orchestrated rock band rehearsing. I said to my wife, "I have a feeling that's a Christian rock group in there. Let's stick around until showtime and see."

The number we heard being rehearsed was a recent rock hit tune whose lyrics were filled with promiscuity, so naturally my wife laughed at my assumption. When showtime arrived the announcer said, "And now from --------------University, the ---------- ---------------."

The fact that ------------- --------------- University is a Christian school was never mentioned—undoubtedly to protect the innocent. The introductory song was Cream's big acid-rock hit, "In the Sunshine of Your Love." It contains lyrics with reference to the sex act that are too crude to repeat. Fortunately this was a completely instrumental version.

This group almost out-creamed the Cream. The driving rhythm and brass sections were kept going by not one, but *two* drummers, each with a complete trap set. For the first half-hour of the performance I waited vainly for at least one tame pop message song. No way. Just lots of good old heavy, savage rock.

At one point a young man from the group led the way with uninhibited frenzy in a dance up and down the aisles. Others followed him. I hadn't seen anything like this since I left the Far East where I observed heathen self-mutilation and torture rites which I'll describe in a later chapter.

After the number had ended, the moderator came to the microphone and referred to the lead male dancer by saying, "His grandmother came to see our performance last night and she described her grandson's dancing by saying, 'He's possessed.'" Everybody laughed. But I wonder if perhaps grandma wasn't right.

A couple of additional rock numbers followed, then the moderator returned to the microphone and delivered the punch line: "I suppose you wonder why we're here. We're here to tell you of our personal faith in God."

36

This statement was followed, believe it or not, by a medley from the musical production "Hair." Next came the only religious song of the evening, "Faith of Our Fathers." The hymn was really more patriotic than spiritual.

I waited in vain to hear about their personal faith in God but no testimony even came close to such an expression. Finally, a couple of rock hits concluded the program. I thought the least they could have done would be to give a plug for their school. They didn't even do that. As the people left, the band members wandered through the audience hawking their record albums.

As I walked up the aisle I inadvertently overheard one of the male singers trying to hustle one of the attractive female members of the audience. My heart found no tears for this group, only righteous indignation. If I had any sorrow at all, it was for the scores of financial contributors back home who had sacrificially given so that these young people could spend their summer on the West Coast "witnessing" for Christ. I would not want to be the one to answer to God on judgment day for such an investment of the Lord's time and money!

chapter four

WHOSE IS

THE WINNING PLAY?

The intent of Christian rock is noble: to bring young people to a saving knowledge of Jesus Christ. Unfortunately, advocates of this approach wrap the message in a promotional package that denies the self-sufficiency of God's Word. They insist that the Gospel needs a boost in its public image so it won't turn off prospective converts. But does the updating of the evangel really work?

Christian rock attempts to con the world by a commercial, Madison Avenue Approach that appeals to the unregenerate masses.

Young people today are tuned into the vibrations of rock. Upon this premise Christian rock makes its approach. Statistics indicate that eighty-seven percent of teenagers today chew, taste and digest a steady diet of rock. [1] The average teen listens to the radio approximately five hours each day. [2]   Advocates of Christian rock insist that their approach to the music-oriented young world is a clever ploy. Their strategy is to take the medium of rock, to which youth is precon-ditioned, and use it to translate the message of Christ. Attract them with rock, they say, then give them God.

"After all," they argue, "you can't win someone to Christ unless you first bring that someone under the sound of the Gospel." Rock is their instrument to gain an audience. When the crowd is gathered with a little rock then the true purpose of the meeting can be revealed. ("Ha, ha! We're Christians after all! Sure fooled you, didn't we?")

Why do we need to hide the Gospel under this cloak of deceit and conformity? Such antics give the rock generation one more reason to criticize the con-game of the Establishment. They're tired of being duped by high-powered advertising techniques. Can Mrs. Olson's coffee really save marriages? Do blondes really have more fun? Is an astronaut really qualified to tell us whether or not we need railroads?

Young people respect someone who is honest and straightforward. Why, then, adopt an approach that they are weary of? Must the Gospel really be commer-cially oriented? Christian rock advocates don't need to sell Jesus. Judas beat them to it!

Almost all Christian rock entertainers think of numbers first and souls second. Everybody wants a crowd. The question remains, however, whether a mass appeal involves a sacrifice of principles.

It's true, a rock concert is more likely to get a crowd than will a sermon. No one really believes that a commune of hippies is going to flock en masse to hear a message of sin and judgment. I rather suspect, however, that if they don't it is not necessarily the fault of the medium or the message. The responsibility might just possibly lie with those who willfully reject God's pardon for sin.

A large audience does not necessarily spell success in any venture. It tells only part of the story. Thousands have enthusiastically attended our anti-rock crusades in recent months, yet the premises of this book cannot be justified on that fact alone. The Apostle Philip could have preached to an entire city, but God chose to guide him to an Ethiopian in a desert and by that strategy eventually introduced an entire continent to the life-changing message of the Gospel.

Many pastors and youth leaders today are in a state of despair. They grope after anything or anyone promising to stop the exodus from the church. Like General Motors each year, they expect a redesign of the product to create a new market. In their desperation to change the package, Christian rock promoters have often altered the contents of the goods. Theological purity has often been sacrificed in order to salvage the diminishing audience.

How then should Christ be presented? Certainly we are to be wise as serpents and do nothing to drive a sinner away without his hearing the Gospel. A negative, self-righteous approach will attract no one. But the antithesis of this extreme is Christian rock which promotes falsehoods by obscuring its intentions. Those who are sincerely ready to turn from their sin are not going to be turned off by an honest gospel presentation. If some are offended and turn away from the preaching of Christ let us remember that the cross has always been offensive to the unregenerate. Our obligation is not first to produce a crowd. It is not to manipulate the message to force results. We must find the middle ground between the rigid, archaic approach of institutionalized Protestantism and the unscriptural con-game of Christian rock.

May God help us to find that place.

Christian rock presents a false perspective of the Christian life by trying to show how groovy it is to be a Christian.

One Christian rock performer once remarked, "I think of Jesus Christ as a rock singer and the church as His public relations agent. I think the latter has done a poor job."

This man was trying to say that he considers Christ relevant today but that the eternal Son of God needs to be dressed up for the now generation. That thinking brings rock into the church with all its gesticulatory, callipygian dance routines. It incorporates hip language and mini fashions in an attempt to sharpen the image of what a Christian is. "See? We're really swingers just like you! Why don't you just turn on to the groovy Christian life?"

Such an approach focuses on the flesh instead of on the spirit. Clothing and choreography will never make the Gospel appealing. Great men of the faith have been martyrs, not swingers. To say simply that the Christian life offers exactly what the world is seeking is a distortion of truth. The world is seeking pleasure and ease. The symbol of the cross is death for the sinner, not just a re-direction of his life. Acts 5:41 declares: "They departed from the presence of the council, rejoicing that they were counted worthy to suffer shame for His name."

Reproach for the sake of Christ is apparently not acceptable to some believers today. Gospel rock promoters try to show that Christ is really a "super hippie."

"Hey, man," they say, "take that eternal trip and turn on with Jesus. You don't have to drop acid. Drop a little Matthew, Mark, Luke and John. It's free and you can score any time and any place without fear of getting busted. God is not only good, He is groovy!"

42

Such an appeal may be more easily understood, but it could obscure the true Christ. It takes more than psychedelic Bible covers, hip language and rock music to lead someone to Christ. He must in the end recognize that his old life has him in the grip of sin and death. He must want the new life and be willing to pay the price of sacrifice to achieve it.

No single form of communication alone makes a man respond to Christ. There is no way to make the Gospel "more relevant." It is the most incredible message in the world. Even the great Apostle Paul was mocked when he declared that Christ was the Son of God and rose from the dead.

First Corinthians 2:14 makes it clear: "The natural man receiveth not the things of the Spirit of God ... they are foolishness unto him; neither can he know them, because they are spiritually discerned." The only way a sinner can believe the Gospel is by the miracle of faith inspired by the Holy Spirit which leads to new birth.

The false perspective of Christian rock is basically a desire for status. Too many evangelicals today crave acceptance and recognition by the world and strive to show that Christians are not inferior, secular citizens. But our work is not to gain the world's attention for selfish reasons. It is to save its soul. To impress your neighbor may not be to save him. The Gospel is not intended to *please* men but to *warn* them. The Apostle Paul declared, "For if I yet pleased men, I should not be the servant of Christ" (Galatians 1:10). When we lock horns in competition with Hollywood and Las Vegas we are only going to make a mockery of the Gospel's true ability to redeem the soul.

The Christian life is indeed exciting. It offers thrilling experiences that lead to joy. But it is hardly "groovy"! Those who serve Christ can testify that discipline and self-denial are more appropriate de-

43

scriptions. The Apostle Paul said, "I die daily" (I Corinthians 15:31), "I am crucified with Christ" (Galatians 2:20), and "I beseech you therefore ... that ye present your bodies a living sacrifice ... unto God" (Romans 12:1).

Jesus said, "If you were of the world, the world would love his own: but because ... I have chosen you out of the world, therefore the world hateth you" (John 15:19). This is the realistic perspective of the Christian life.

Christians are not promised a bed of roses. They are warned to expect trials and trouble. But they are also promised an inner strength and a higher hope to overcome those difficulties. Jesus gives us reality, not the pseudo-contentment of a "trip." The approach of Christian rock may be dazzling, but in the long run an honest, realistic presentation of Christ will prove to be more effective.

Christian rock songs focus on ambiguous ideals of love, peace and philosophical humanism while neglecting to emphasize man's sinfulness and his need of salvation.

Christian rock advocates try to convince us that the lyrics of most church songs today are outdated. They suggest that the young rock generation needs a Gospel in the language of the vernacular to communicate effectively. Above all, Christian rock promoters stress that lyrics should not offend the sinner. "Separation from God," they reason, is a phrase that is just as forceful as the old-fashioned word "hell."

There are some who suggest a more indirect, subliminal approach in the lyrics. Consequently, many Christian rock songs are devised merely to raise questions and create moods for the listener. It is supposed that even without hearing biblical truths listeners will draw the proper spiritual conclusions eventually.

44

Abstractionism has little effect in communicating the Gospel. There is no virtue in continually raising questions without denoting a clear-cut answer. The subliminal approach may be fine for selling toothpaste, but "faith comes by hearing, and hearing by the Word of God." More than psychological trickery must be considered in evangelism. "We wrestle not against flesh and blood, but against principalities, against powers, against the rulers of the darkness of this world" (Ephesians 6:12).

In presenting the Gospel, simplicity is more of a virtue than ambiguity. Listeners must plainly understand our message and purpose. Ambiguity may be useful in the initial contact but ultimately spiritual truth must be clearly explained. Much Christian rock is guilty of beginning ambiguously and ending in the same way.

The lyrics of church music must be theologically and scripturally supportable. Unfortunately, many Christian rock songs fail this test. Some are outright anti-scriptural (e.g. "Spirit in the Sky," mentioned earlier).

There is a trend in Christian rock toward borrowing secular pop and rock songs and offering them as a representation of the Christian viewpoint. This angle was observed first in the days of songs such as "I Believe" ("For every drop of rain a flower grows" is hardly a doctrinal statement of Christian faith), and "He" ("He'll *always* say, 'I forgive'" — that's unscriptural unless accompanied by the explanation that repentance is required first).

This search for Christian themes in secular songs is ridiculous. Some recent examples include: "Everything Is Beautiful." The lyrics suggest that man, if given time, will find an answer to his problems. This song expresses humanism, not faith in the transforming power of Christ. "Try a Little Kindness" is romantic

45

sentimentalism that falls far short of Ephesians 4:32. "Bridge Over Troubled Waters" is a pretty melody but the dependence expressed is on the arm of man, not God. "People Gotta Be Free" is a song originally written not to express freedom of spirit for work and worship and disciplined love. Rather, it is a pitch for the permissive and morally anarchistic life-style of the hippies. "He Ain't Heavy He's My Brother" is philosophical idealism but it comes far short of I Peter 5:7 and Matthew 11:28-30. I am not condemning these songs, but only trying to show that they are poor substitutes for the Gospel. If it works to his advantage, satan will inject half truths and high ideals into pop and rock music. But he will never permit the unmitigated essence of the Gospel to be explicitly proclaimed.

Several youth-oriented musical productions are available for youth choirs looking to rock. Such musicals range in lyric and rhythmic content from spiritually shallow blubbering to blasphemous outrage. For an interesting analysis, take one of those Christian youth musicals and count the number of times pronouns such as "He," "Him," "Someone," and "Somebody" are used instead of the names "God," "Jesus," "Jesus Christ," or "Christ." Note also how few times the themes of the blood atonement, repentance, the crucifixion, the Second Coming are mentioned.

When I applied this analysis to a well-known Christian rock musical I derived the following totals: blood—0; cross—4 (all in one song); sin—0; hell—0; judgment—0; righteousness—0; Christ—1; Jesus Christ —1. God was mentioned only once in the first eleven songs and Jesus was not mentioned until the eighteenth song.

The foregoing totals are evidence of the musical's pathetic weakness especially in view of the fact that this presentation contains twenty-one songs! This production is typical of so much Christian rock. The songs are witness to subjective, temporal emotions rather than to eternal, objective truth.

Colossians 3:16 admonishes the believer to follow certain spiritual directives in worship. We are to sing in "psalms and hymns and spiritual songs." The "psalms" may be classified as songs of praise. "Hymns" would describe most traditional church music containing statements of faith or petitions addressed to God in prayer. "Spiritual songs" are those with exhortations and witness that testify to the faithfulness of Christ. Most acceptable gospel songs fall into the last category. Since most Christian rock songs fit none of these classifications it is difficult to see what scriptural basis they have for use in the church.

If Christ were to walk into one of the "worship" services currently being staged for youth with their rock music, strobe lights, flashing slogans and psychedelic art He might well declare: "Take these things away. My house shall be called a house of prayer, but you have made it a den of psychedelic self-indulgence!"

The basic problem with the ambiguity and philosophical ideals in Christian rock lyrics is that they usually contain just enough spiritual truth to make the listener feel comfortably religious, but not enough to convict him and lead him to salvation. Christian rock promoters comfort themselves by believing that their lyrical messages are moral, positive, and full of hope. Such content, however, is not sufficient for a genuine gospel presentation. One need not dwell constantly on King James prose, of course. But whatever terminology is used should be explicit and completely understandable to the audience to which it is directed.

Too frequently Christian rock is over-weighted toward the problem of man's moral dilemmas without a clear explanation of the solution in Christ. The

Gospel is a directive to the cross. Christian lyrics may create a mood, but they should always convey a message that is theologically sound.

Christian rock identifies with the same life and music styles of the rock culture with an "add Jesus to your bag" philosophy that offers no alternative to those who are fed up with that style of living.

To convince followers that their Christian life is attractive, most entertainers in Christian rock surround themselves with the subcultural trappings of bizarre life styles. The idea is to be relevant by identifying with the subculture that they are trying to reach for Christ.

In my talks with rock enthusiasts I have discovered that some of them, though certainly not all, even carry the identification to the extreme of espousing the typical anti-authoritarian and anti-American philosophies of the rock culture. Those who are pro-Christian rock insist they would be rejected if they looked and sounded straight. They argue that, even as members of the Establishment are turned off by long hair and the frenzied beat of rock, so "their" peers would be turned off by the short-haired straights who like sedate forms of music. In gross misinterpretation of I Corinthians 9:22 they justify their dress and music styles. The scriptural passage declares: "I am made all things to all men, that I might by all means save some."

One Christian rock singer expressed his philosophy in terms of sheer compromise: "We're trying to give them a message through a medium which they like and understand. Through our music we are showing people it is possible to live a normal life and be a Christian too. You don't have to be a wierdo and live in a box somewhere never having anything to do with the world around you, even if you do believe in God."

This type of justification is an example of the sort that suggests, "add Jesus to your bag." The idea is that the Christian life requires no real changes in your forms of pleasure and entertainment. You can keep your same hair style, musical tastes, and social and political philosophies. The change occurs only on the inside. Christian rock advocates insist that II Corinthians 5:17, declaring that if any man is in Christ he is a "new creation," applies only to the spiritual regeneration that takes place and that any changes in outward style are meaningless—culturally related to a specific era. Whether clothes are mod or straight, whether hair is long or short, one thing is certain: the overriding biblical principle is moderation.

Those who are genuinely converted to Christ usually detest their former life with its hopelessness and despair. Among those who have been involved with the hippie, drug and rock music scene, there is a feeling of dread in looking back—and a revulsion that extends to Christian rock. Although this reaction is not always true, many no longer wish to sound, act or look like the world they left behind.

Before adopting the life and music styles of the rock generation, Christian promoters of rock should stop and think about the attitudes of the secular world toward rock. Although they may be accused of being part of the Establishment, most adults (even non-Christians) reject the hippie life-style and the wild beat of rock. The majority of the principals with whom I have talked while appearing in hundreds of schools each year are very much anti-rock. Their position is probably based on cultural and practical reasons instead of spiritual considerations. But the point is that many sinners reject rock. How can such antics bring glory to God when sinners themselves see professing Christians adopting the same approach? The secular world is passing legislation against rockfests. The secular world is devising court injunctions to prevent the assembling of young people to groove on pot and rock. Such well-known personalities as Art Linkletter and Spiro Agnew have taken public positions against rock. The point is clear: These men represent a majority of opinion of the adult world.

People around the entire globe recognize the moral debauchery of rock. Their outrage has been so great that anti-obscenity clauses are now being written into the contracts of most rock bands. Whenever they make U. S. appearance the promoters and concert hall managers require that the bands post a cash bond that they are to forfeit if there is an "illegal, indecent, profane, lewd or immoral exhibition" while the group is on stage. [3]

The trend of safeguarding public morals started after the Jim Morrison caper in Miami in 1969. In Denver, concert promoters required a $10,000 bond thirty days in advance of a concert. It is obvious that even the world associates obscenity and lewdness with rock music. Is this not a sufficient reason for not wishing to identify with such a phenomenon?

When Moses and Joshua descended from Mount Sinai with the tablets of stone the Bible says in Exodus 32:17-18, "When Joshua heard the noise of the people as they shouted he said unto Moses, there is a noise of war in the camp."

Moses, however, arrived at a different interpretation: "It is not the voice of them that shout for mastery, neither is it the voice of them that cry for being overcome: but the noise of them that sing do I hear."

The point is, Moses heard a certain type of music and immediately drew a conclusion about what was happening. He recognized that it was not the music and sound of victory or defeat in battle. All this points out that even in the day of Moses certain musical idioms accompanied specific types of conduct.

The associations of rock have nothing to do with the attributes of the Christian faith. Therefore, to use this musical idiom is to identify with the morally negative characteristics rock represents. Is rock therefore even a reasonable vehicle with which to identify when presenting Christ?

We must face the fact that identification is not regeneration. In their lack of stress on outward change in coming to Christ, some Christian rock advocates are trying to put the robe on the prodigal while he is still feeding on husks. If anyone does, certainly the church ought to have something different to offer the world than what it has already. The new order should be not only a regenerated inner life but a change in outward attributes as well. If one sincerely follows Christ he will not want to bring reproach on the Gospel by assuming a life style that much of the world itself rejects.

I have discovered that the majority of those in rock and drug cultures who are ready to turn to Christ are doing so because they've reached a dead-end street. They recognize that such a frenzied life cannot bring lasting satisfaction. They want an alternative.

One recent example testifies to this fact. A hippie and his girl friend were present in one of our crusades. When the invitation was given both of them responded to the opportunity to come to Christ. The young man had hair that was longer than any I'd ever seen on a male. Both were dressed in typical hippie garb. After a period of extensive prayer and counseling I talked to them about the importance of coming out from the world to serve Christ. They expressed no opposition to my stand against rock music. During the course of our conversation I asked, "Why would someone such as yourself who had been deep into the drug and rock music scene come out to a church service to hear a sermon knocking both?"

51

The young man answered: "I had tried that scene and knew that what I was looking for couldn't be found there. So I thought if you were knocking rock that you might have a better answer."

I fear that if the evangelical church continues to adopt rock life and music styles there may come a day when large portions of this Protestant classification will have nothing to offer those who are sick of the rock scene. Shouldn't we be able to give people something different? I thank God for those concerned believers who refuse to attempt to reach the young by "relevance" and "identification" schemes. Those who have a burden to reach unchurched youth should simply be honest. Many are sick of the rock scene. They want an antedote, not another pill of the same fruitless experimentation.

chapter five

THE FILTH
AND THE
FURY

Since many performers involved in Christian rock admit that its image is questionable, how can they justify their participation in it?

They insist that they are applying this medium within a Christian frame of reference and ask that judgment be reserved until they have had time to prove the validity of their actions.

The danger here is that the ministry of reaching souls should not be conducted on the basis of trial and error. God's will must constantly be sought and each step guided by both compassion and reason. How we apply the truth of the Gospel will determine to a large degree whether or not the sinner sees them in proper perspective. When all is said and done, Christian rock is on shaky ground.

Christian rock denies the biblical injunction of II Cor-
inthians 6:17-18 ("be ye separate") and admits it draws
no line of distinction between the secular and the
sacred.

Liberals have encouraged an increasingly secular role for the church in the past several decades. They have given precedence to political and social causes over spiritual concerns. Evangelicals who wouldn't think of matching the record of the liberals in such secular activity have been trapped into doing just that through Christian rock. This type of music makes little distinction between religious and non-religious music styles. In fact, the very terms "sacred" and "secular" are considered non-applicable to musical idioms.

"Music is music," Christian rock enthusiasts insist. Consequently they place the world and the church on the same level in this realm.

Many Christian rock concerts use hard rock techniques to accompany supposedly Christian lyrics in addition to secular rock songs that have been hits on the record sales charts. Both types are interwoven seemingly without discretion. The strategy is to attract the world with familiar rock sounds and songs while at the same time showing sinners how much the world and the church have in common. Christian rock promoters reason that rock as a musical style is morally neutral. Using this technique, they say, does not constitute a secularization of the ministry. If they admit that there is some rottenness in rock they minimize it, calculating that the good outweighs the bad and the bad is but satan's misuse of what is simply the "now sound of youth."

I maintain that the use of Christian rock is a blatant compromise so obvious that only those who are spiritually blind by carnality can accept it. Christ has called us out of the world. Compromise in satan's territory is dangerous. But my warning often gets this reply: "Don't be a fanatic. Get where the action is! After all, you are 'salt' and by being near the world you can understand it better."

The compromise of Christian rock involves an "easy believism." It suggests that becoming a Christian is really quite easy. As a result, many churches are filled with young people who are culturally little different from the pagans of the city in which they live. They have never made a clean break with the world and see no need to do so.

More than a semantic definition separates the terms sacred and secular. The Old Testament makes this clear. The laws of Leviticus strictly distinguished certain activities as religious and others as non-religious. Today, as New Testament believers, we have Christ living in us. With that constantly in mind we should "do all to the glory of God" (I Corinthians 10:31). There are, however, certain specific activities which relate to the church in such a way as to be categorized as sacred.

Any fusion of secular methods with sacred intentions is in danger of becoming a truce with the world. Any attempt to draw parallels of similarities between the world and the church is a contradiction of Scripture. The true message of the Gospel is an ultimatum: "Repent or perish." Christians need not renounce all pleasures of the secular world, but a clean break must be made with the works of darkness.

An increasing number of gospel-singing groups (even some which do not feature rock music) have been including secular hits on their programs. They sing, for example, "He Touched Me," and follow up with "The Impossible Dream." They argue that as long as the lyrics of a song express a moralistic thought a Christian audience will accept them.

Another phenomenon is the rise of Christian television spectaculars and youth musicals a' la Broadway. Their composition has often been more than one-half secularized. How about the investment of God's time and money in such extravaganzas? Who really is convinced that the world can be won by a show that Hollywood could do better?

Let us suppose that the music is not rock. Even so, if the lyrics and the context are secular it is still not Gospel. Therefore, what can it really contribute? To secularize the Gospel is not only a compromise but also unwise competition as well.

J. S. Bach, once said, "The aim and final reason of all music should be nothing else but the glory of God and the refreshment of the spirit." With an aim like this in mind, how can the use of Christian rock be justified at all?

The secularization of Christian rock is partly a result of frustrated musicians and writers who lack the ability to make it in the secular world. They anchor in the Christian rock harbor to promote what the world has enough discrimination to reject. In most instances, Christian rock isn't even "good" rock. It's usually a cheap imitation. Unfortunately, some Christians are so gullible that they are willing to accept such second-rate material.

My reaction to Christian rock musicians is, "If you want to play rock, why not go into the world where you belong?" If I really want rock I'll go to the Fillmore or Electric Circus and get the real thing from musicians who not only know *what* they are doing but *why* they're doing it.

Many times before Sunday morning or evening services I have knelt with pastors and prayed that the Holy Spirit would anoint and bless the choir's ministry of music. I have never been backstage with a Christian rock group before their concerts so I don't know how they pray. But I wonder: "If the program is to include secular rock numbers, how can one pray for the Holy Spirit to anoint that which was written with intentions and purposes totally at war with the program of God?" There is a wealth of great historic and contemporary (non-rock) church music available for presenting the Gospel in song. We really don't need the world's help. In fact, we would be better off without it. Christian rock is the last straw in the evangelical church's secularization of the Gospel. Let us pray that this vicious parasite will not sap the energy of the churches until they can no longer turn to the work to which they are called.

Christian rock uses the beat and the sound which even the secular world associates with promiscuous sex.

More than any other single thing, the beat of rock has given it such wide appeal. Upon this captivating force Christian rock also has based its approach. The reasoning is that if the beat of rock can captivate the ear of youth for a secular message, why not use it to catch the ear of unsaved youth for a Christian message? Sensing the overwhelming musical appeal of rock they reason that it is too dynamic a force to ignore. Its impact should be utilized.

To charges that rock is often associated with immorality they reply that the effects of beats and rhythms are culturally and historically relative. Those who oppose the involvement of rock rhythms for presenting the Gospel, they suggest, are oldsters tuned in to a different generation. These times move to the beat of a different drummer. And, they say, if we are not to be immediately tuned out, we must change our church idiom.

Time magazine described a performance at Woodstock by the hard rock group Ten Years After as a "rhythmic orgasm." [1]   That's pretty strong language to describe rock, especially by writers of a purely secular periodical.

John Kay of Steppenwolf described his group's success by saying, "One of the reasons we're so successful is that we're able to keep the music hard and direct so that it communicates directly with the body." [2]

A rock-musician friend of mine who had a million-selling rock hit several years ago once discussed with me the eroticism of rock. "My favorite trick," he said, "is to slowly unbutton my shirt until my bare chest completely shows. Then I take off my shirt and throw it into the audience and lie on the floor with the microphone stand and go into sexual postures. I can make the girls do anything I want them to when I'm singing."

Frank Zappa once wrote an extensive article in *Life* magazine on the role of rock in the socio-sexual revolution.   His conclusions were, "Rock music is sex. The big beat matches the body's rhythms." [3]   The former manager of the Rolling Stones once stated precisely the same thing. So did Arthur Brown of "I am the God of Hellfire" fame. [4]

Jerry Rubin, the yippie revolutionary, has this to say in his book, *Do It* (commenting on the history of rock): "Elvis killed Eisenhower by turning our uptight young awakening bodies around. Hard animal rock energy/ beat surged hot through us, the driving rhythm arousing repressed passion. Rock and roll marked the begining of the revolution." [5]

I could go on for many pages with similar statements equating rock with promiscuous sex—all from the secular world. If even a few rock musicians viewed rock in this way it would be a sufficient indictment of guilt by association. When most secular people view rock in this perspective it is a point of disgrace that some in the church cannot see what the world readily discerns.

The use of the beat of rock hardly seems fitting in light of the admonitions of II Corinthians 7:1: "Having therefore these promises, dearly beloved, let us cleanse ourselves from all filthiness of the flesh and spirit, perfecting holiness in the fear of God."

The term "rock and roll" was coined by a Cleveland disc jockey who borrowed the phrase from the ghetto where it was used as a descriptive sex expression. "Rock and roll" actually means "promiscuous sexual relationship music." In this perspective, how does "Christian rock" sound?

The question must be settled: Is rock just another form of music or is it a unique phenomenon with purposes and effects so alienated from the Christian faith that it has no use as a religious vehicle? We are conditioned through our environment to respond in specific ways to certain musical modes, such as tranquilizing music to rest and marches to inject enthusiasm. Since the purpose of church music could generally be agreed to be worship, exhortation, dedication, and testimony, our task is to consider what musical idioms are consistent with such intents. One needs but spend five minutes at a rock concert to see that the purposes of such an endeavor are at moral opposites with the desired effects in the worship and praise of God. If it is necessary to explain that one's intent in using Christian rock is not that of secular rock (as some Christian enthusiasts do) it seems that the applying of new meanings to the style of rock is stretching credibility too far.

The message of rock runs parallel with a permissive attitude toward sex, drugs and revolution, to say nothing of the questionable personal lives of those who perform rock and the environment in which they work. In this perspective it seems that the world may be correct in its use of rock while the Christians in rock may be completely wrong.

At this point it should be admitted that one doesn't need to be stuffy by insisting on staid anthems for church music. They do not always communicate effectively to those who have not learned to appreciate such musical forms. But why scrape the gutter at the other end of the musical spectrum and use rock? I am not seeking to endorse or perpetuate any particular musical form. But youth-oriented church music certainly needs a great deal more prayerful discretion applied than has been evident in some quarters.

Recently I witnessed the dramatic conversion of a young radio announcer who had been committed to Christian rock. His testimony is an encouragement to those who yearn to see musically involved Christian young people take a stand against rock. The young man works for a Christian radio station and in fact was helping to formulate a partial Christian rock format for the station. He had also been offered a job by a soft drink corporation to do an underground (secular) rock radio show that would be syndicated all across the nation.

After attending one of our crusades he destroyed more than five hundred dollars worth of hard rock albums he had purchased. In an open letter he wrote to me expressing his feelings. Those who are committed to Christian rock should heed the advice of this experienced D. J.:

> When I started listening to rock I found that I liked it. I started buying rock albums and I could almost feel the beat in my blood. I was slowly becoming addicted to it. But I was a Christian. I even built my own stereo

60

room to be surrounded by sound. I could seldom get enough of hard, progressive rock.

I knew that rock had strong influencial powers and I reasoned that maybe it could be used to spread the Gospel and I stood firm in those feelings. What I wouldn't admit was that I couldn't worship the Lord while I was hearing those drums and other instruments pound out the rhythm. I felt the driving sound and rhythm in my body and mind. It was a flesh trip. Logic tells me that if one is going to worship the Lord one should have his mind on the Lord ... not on the feeling you're getting from that groovy Christian music. I believe in making a joyful noise unto the Lord but when the music leaves the spiritual realm and becomes a driving force it goes into the physical realm ... a realm that takes worship away from God and puts the music to work satisfying one's self.

When I heard Bob Larson I knew that it was time for me to forget the physical satisfaction found in something that was not given of God and it was time for me to remember the spiritual satisfactions that were found in God.

If I'm fighting to win a spiritual war I cannot voluntarily listen to the enemy's propaganda.

Very Sincerely,
A *Newer Creature in Christ*

I pray that as more young people become disillusioned about Christian rock they will be willing to separate themselves from it. I invite all young people sincerely concerned with reaching their generation for the Savior not to be sold short by the spiritually superficial and self-aggrandizing efforts of most Christian rock promoters. Wake up, lest you become a blind follower of the blind and both of you fall into the ditch!

When used excessively, under proper circumstances, the beat of rock is a force accommodating demonic possession and therefore is not worthy as a vehicle to communicate the Gospel.

In previous chapters of this book I have first stated the position of Christian rock before presenting my objections. In this section I will depart from that approach because there is really no Christian rock antithesis for my next charge against the use of rock as a religious vehicle. In fact, Christian rock fans with whom I have conversed either totally disregard or openly ridicule the premise of this section, that mere music can lead to the excess of courting evil spirits.

The argument is developed fully in my book, *Rock & Roll: the Devil's Diversion,* from which the following is taken.

Dr. Franzblau, noted New York psychiatrist, has observed, "Many of these dances are really the modern version of the tribal dances, and dancing is body language ... Of course many of these dances ... may be a way of wooing and courting the foreplay to love making." [6] Dr. Barnard Saible, child guidance expert of the Washington State division of community services, stated in *The Seattle Times,* "Normally recognizable girls behaved (at a rock and roll concert) as if possessed by some demonic urge, defying in emotional ecstasy the restraint which authorities try to place on them."

The Encyclopaedia Britannica says, "The therapeutic possession dances of Africa have spread to the new world. ... In these dances an African diety enters a devotee and produces a frenzied dance in the character of the god." [7]

Could any statement be plainer? Is not the trend from less skillful maneuvering in dancing to more rhythmic forms representative of demonic influence?

Early American settlers followed the dancing examples set by Europeans. The innovations that were to come were derived from the Negro, who has had a greater creative incluence on music and dancing than any other ethnic group. The origin of this Negro influence was, of course, Africa. These innovations were connected with heathen tribal and voodoo rites. The native dances to incessant, pulsating, syncopated rhythms until he enters a state of hypnotic monotony and loses active control over his conscious mind. The throb of the beat from the drums brings his mind to a state when the voodoo, which Christian missionaries know to be demon, can enter him. This power then takes control of the dancer, usually resulting in sexual atrocities. Is there a legitimate connection between these religious rites and today's modern dances?

Because of our technologically oriented society, universal determinism and inductive reasoning are very prevalent in the thought processes of people today. Our educational system is based upon accepting only those facts which can be observed and investigated. The twentieth century mind thinks in terms of scientific procedure and controlled experiments, and therefore has difficulty in accepting the existence of spiritual entities on an empirical basis. A study of demonology is usually relegated to the ranks of superstition; however, a recent resurgence of interest in clairvoyance, astrology and ESP has given popular credibility to the reality of supernatural factors and events in life. Taking this into account, it is my hope that the readers of this book will not reject the ensuing discussion without serious consideration.

Any intelligent discussion of the little-understood subject of demonology should begin with a definition of terms. A demon may be regarded as a spirit being not discernable through the five physical senses. It is not necessary to argue for their existence as this is universally accepted in all religions. Pagan religions, which believe in the reincarnation of spirits, are based on "mysteries and oracles," from the tower of Babel on down to the present. The Bible gives a broad outline of this subject, referring to it as "the mystery of iniquity."

Lucifer's fall, as set forth in the fourteenth chapter of Isaiah and the fourth chapter of Jeremiah and the twenty-eighth chapter of Ezekiel, marks the origin of evil in this universe. Since his fall, he is referred to in Holy Writ as "Satan, the old Devil, and the god of this world." One writer indicated that as many as one-third of the angels of heaven joined Lucifer in his initial rebellion. [8]

Man is prey to these fallen creatures. They are regimented into legions dwelling in regions of the deep. They assail men for possession of their faculties. Through men they find expression for their diabolical purpose of deposing and discrediting God. Those who consort with spirits are known as witches, wizards, or warlocks. Their occult communication with these fallen creatures is established in elaborate rituals. An array of pagan gods stands on the ruins of history, shrouded in fear and superstition, still holding strange gravity even in this enlightened age.

Christ came to earth to deal with men's problems on a personal level. He revealed to men that demons of blindness, deafness, and spirits of infirmity were holding them prisoner. Satan had accomplished this by an infusion of his power into the very nature of men. The New Testament contains many instances in which

64

Christ utilized exorcism. "Cast out devils," Jesus said to the seventy as He sent them out. Matthew, the tenth chapter, and the Great Commission of Mark, the sixteenth chapter, contain the same commandment. There are also instances (such as in the fifth and ninth chapters of Mark) when demons spoke and uttered cries. During the revival at Samaria under Phillip's ministry it is stated that unclean spirits cried with loud voices and came out of many. Sacred Scripture accounts for many strange emotional and physical actions as the tormented souls were set free from inner bondage. Once, the victim wallowed, foaming at the mouth while another was "torn" and still others seemed to lie in a trance with their eyes glazed in a semi-conscious stupor. Either Christ was a superstitious liar and the Bible is a collection of fables, or we must accept the reality of the existence of demons and their capability of possessing men.

I Timothy 4:1 declares: "The Spirit speaketh expressly that in the latter times many shall depart from the faith, giving heed to seducing spirits and doctrines of demons."

I was aware of the connection between demons and dancing even before my conversion. I speak from experience as to the effect rock and roll rhythms have on the mind. When you perform at a dance, the songs do not last two or three minutes, as they might on a recording. Instead, you learn to control your crowd by the music that you play. I have played one song continuously for as long as fifteen to twenty minutes. There were times while playing rock and roll music, that I became so engrossed and my senses so deadened, that I was hardly aware of what was going on about me. As a minister, I know now what it is like to feel the unction of the Holy Spirit. As a rock musician, I knew what it meant to feel the counterfeit anointing of Satan.

I am not alone in my experimental knowledge of the influence of demonic powers present in rock music. One of the most uncanny stories I have ever heard was related to me by a close friend of mine who works among the hippies. For several weeks he dealt with a sixteen-year-old boy who by his own admission communed with demon spirits. One day he asked my friend to turn on the radio to a rock station. As they listened, this teenager related, just prior to the time the singer on the recording would sing them, the words to songs he had never heard before. When asked how he could do this the sixteen-year-old replied that the same demon spirits that he was acquainted with had inspired the songs. Also, he explained, that while on acid trips he could hear demons sing some of the very songs he would later hear recorded by acid-rock groups.

Many "heavy" rock groups write their songs while under the influence of drugs. Some of them admit to receiving the inspiration for songs from a power that seems to control them. In 1968 Ginger Baker, the drummer for The Cream, was interviewed concerning his emotional feelings while he performed. He replied, "It happens to us quite often—it feels as though I'm not playing my instrument, something else is playing it and that same thing is playing all three of our instruments (referring to the rest of the group). That's what I mean when I say it's frightening sometimes. Maybe we'll all play the same phrase out of nowhere. It happens very often with us". [9]

Joe Cocker, a top rock singer, goes through grotesque contortions as he performs. His fingers make obscene gestures, his mouth contorts, and his eyes bulge as if he had muscular dystrophy combined with St. Vitus' Dance. He described his performances to *Time* by saying that when he sings rock something "seizes" him. [10]

In a similar vein, before his death Jimi Hendrix admitted he had visions and communed with spirits. [11] Are these statements related when they refer to a supernatural power in rock that can grip both performer and listener?

There is no difference between the repetitive movements of witch doctors and tribal dancers and the dances of American teenagers. The same coarse bodily motions which lead African dancers into a state of uncontrolled frenzy are present in modern dances. It is only logical, then that there must also be a correlation in the potentiality of demons gaining possessive control of a person through the medium of the beat. This is not entirely my own theory. It is the message that missionaries have urged me to bring to the American public. Many have told me of their exasperation at being sent to foreign lands to save people from what is going on in America's teenage dances. I have observed teenagers frantically gyrate for hours to primitive rhythms until they nearly droped from exhaustion. Such scenes bear such a singular resemblance to heathendom that they cannot be dismissed without pondering the social and moral implications.

Not long ago I traveled on an around-the-world missionary evangelism tour. This afforded me an opportunity to view firsthand the demon possession rites of pagan religions. In Singapore I observed *Thaipusam,* a penance and self-mutilation rite of Hinduism. (For more information, consult the author's book, *Hippies, Hindus and Rock & Roll.*) With knives, skewers, pins, hooks, and spears the Hindus pierced their bodies. While all of this was taking place an incessant, pulsating rhythm was maintained by the musicians. The drummer kept a primitive beat going for hours so that those being tortured could be kept in the proper state of mind.

Those who were not being tortured were watching or dancing. Dozens of teens gyrated wildly, going through the same sensual gesticulations that I had observed in the dances of American teenagers. The rhythm of the music was the same pulsating and syncopated tempo used in hard rock. What has happening here in Singapore can be observed in most teenage dances in America.

Suddenly one of the teenagers screamed. His body became stiff and he fell to the ground, writhing and kicking. It took four men to hold him steady. Other teenagers who had been dancing began to suffer the same symptoms.

"What's happening?" I yelled to a man standing nearby.

"We dance to this kind of music until the spirit of our god enters into us," he answered.

I watched, somewhat frightened now, as one teenager after another screamed and was torn by convulsions under the influence of demon powers. The stimulus of the beat had been used as a medium to put them in a state of mind whereby demons could enter into them.

I realize that what I shall state in this paragraph is very controversial, but I am firmly convinced of its veracity. The day is approaching when one-half of America's population will be comprised of youth. Satan knows that if he is to be effective in these last days before the imminent return of Christ he must gain control of youth. Hard rock is the agency which Satan is using to possess this generation *en masse*. I have seen with my own eyes teenagers who have become demon-possessed while dancing to rock music. It was particularly noticeable with girls. One might expect a young lady to maintain some decency while dancing, but I have seen teenage girls go through contortions that could only be the manifestation of demon activity.

It used to strike fear in my heart when I would see these things happen as they danced to my music. A demon does not have to stay in a person if he does not find that one permanently advantageous to his purposes; however, as that person gives himself over to the of rock and roll, the demon may momentarily enter, do moral and spiritual devestation, and then leave again.

On Friday and Saturday nights across America the the devil is gaining demonic control over thousands of teenage lives. It is possible that any person who has danced for substantial lengths of time to rock music may have come under the oppressive, obsessive, or possessive influence of demons. Knowing this, churches and clergymen need to shed their cloak of compromise and firmly denounce rock and roll dances. Dancing is no longer an artistic form of expression (if it ever was) but a subtle instrument of Satan to morally and spiritually destroy youth.

If Christian rock advocates admit that under some circumstances rock might be involved in eliciting demon possession should not they avoid entirely this musical medium? There is no neutral ground. If they will agree only in part with the position I have presented their obvious course of action should be to reject the use of rock as a vehicle to communicate the Gospel. Once the possibility of demon involvement is suggested, there is no way Christian rock can be justified.

Christian rock is an attempt to give young people what they want rather than what they need while catering to their immative spiritual values and undeveloped musical tastes.

There can be no argument that youth is tuned in to rock—many Christian kids included. Christian rock

69

operates on the excuse that since Christian teens like rock we ought therefore to adopt it as a church music style that will be more appealing to youth. To anyone who might object the advocates of Christian rock excitedly explain that contemporary youth must be understood and given what they want. Any anti-rock statement by an adult over thirty is interpreted as a lack of evangelistic compassion and an attempt to perpetuate the "antiquated" musical Establishment of the church. Some church music directors widen the rift between generations by stating that Christian rock has brought new interest and involvement on the part of teenagers who before had been turned off by the more traditional hymns.

Because of my age and work among young people, no one can construe this indictment as being anti-youth. I meet and talk with thousands of teenagers in my crusades in all corners of America and have found many of them far more dedicated to Christ than their elders. Yet I am appalled by what I discern to be an alarming increase in the spiritual instability of most young people. Their hunger for rock is due partly to their spiritual immaturity. Rock makes an appeal to the physical and the carnal. Those who live superficial lives spiritually will obviously gravitate quickly to such an approach. This, of course, is by no means true in all cases. There are some involved in Christian rock whose sincerity and spirituallity is genuine.

Not only are many young people immature spiritually, but musically as well. When I denounce rock the typical response of this kind of teen is, "But what else is there to listen to?" They act as though rock were the only music in the world. For their tastes, that's often a fact! Some teenagers hear nothing but rock. Their appetite for other styles of music is underdeveloped. If I suggest other kinds of music they often reply, "But that kind of music is dead. Besides, I don't like it."

Rock has oriented these teens to "body" music and they can't appreciate "head" music. It is natural for teenagers to look, act, and think like their associates. Many Christians are included among those teens who have never broadened their musical horizons to include any fresh form of musical enjoyment.

For this dearth of musical fare the church must share the blame. The church has been a cultural center for the fine arts through the centuries. In our time it has bowed to modern pop culture. The role of the church ought still to be one of cultural as well as spiritual leadership of men who are transformed by Christ. Instead, the evangelical church today often merely parrots the latest trends in its attempt to "be where it's at."

Too often in this pleasure-mad world the church has attempted to give people what they want in order to entertain them. In recent decades we have seen musical forms introduced which have "Christian" entertainment as their purpose. Some church leaders have accepted as inevitable the premise that church music should entertain first, with the spiritual by-products following naturally. The entertainment then, hopefully, becomes a means of evangelism.

The agony of Calvary is hardly an entertaining fact. Rock, which entertains by arousing the listener sexually, seems extremely ill-fitted to be clothed by the Gospel, although in most instances rock becomes a cloak for the Gospel.

Without intending to offend any Christian brother or sister I must point out that some gospel quartets have deliberately led us down this road of fruitless entertainment. I am not speaking of those sincere, dedicated Christian singing groups who desire to lift up Christ. I am speaking of those to whom gospel singing is completely a commercial enterprise and whose lives are a reproach to the church. A "gospel sing" often resembles a nightclub more than a gathering of saints. Visit the smoke-filled halls and you'll find a covey of women fawning over the singers with whom they have sexually identified because of cheap stage theatrics combined with a rock beat.

Many Christians would be shocked if they knew that some of the more popular quartets are comprised of alcoholics and adulterers! To these singers, the Gospel is a product to sell. They blatantly sandwich in church concerts between nightclub appearances. This is not merely a personal opinion but a concern that has often been expressed to me by consecrated quartets who have appeared in concerts with such groups. Those on the gospel singing circuit who stay true to Christ are much to be admired.

Unfortunately, many teenagers become hooked on rock because they heard it first from a gospel quartet. I can understand the dilemma of Christian teenagers who parents denounce rock while holding on to their wild quartet records. I am not implying that all "lively" quartet records are rock, but some of the more recent releases are and should be avoided by gospel music enthusiasts.

The deplorable state of church music today can be described by Galations 6:8: "For he that soweth to his flesh shall of the flesh reap corruption." For at least three decades we have sowed to the flesh in church music. Rock (the epitomy of carnality) was the inevitable result. There has been little spiritual discernment to reject rock because the church has too often been fed milk instead of meat. Paul declared in Romans 7:18, "In my flesh dwelleth no good thing." When Christian rock advocates give teenagers rock because they want it they are accommodating the baser desires of those who are spiritually impotent.

Today, the attitude of adults toward youth is often to "listen" rather than "lead." A personal illustration affords an excellent example. Those who have read the author's book *Hippies, Hindus, and Rock & Roll* know of my concern over the current influx of Oriental religions into America. Not long ago, on a well-known radio talk show in a large American city, I debated for two hours with the two major stateside representatives of the Maharishi Mahesh Yogi. My partner (chosen by the moderator) in the debate is pastor of one of the largest fundamental churches in the country. The debate was planned to be evenly matched but I soon had to oppose not only the Hindu devotees but the gospel preacher as well. Every attempt of mine to equate transcendental meditation with pagan demonism was met with opposition from my preacher debate partner. When I would attempt to present a Christian perspective he would intervene with, "Let's hear what the Maharishi's representatives have to say."

Several days after the debate a minister friend of mine wrote my debate partner expressing disappointment at this failure to denote the sharp scriptural distinction between the Gospel and the pagan pantheism of transcendental meditation. His reply in a letter is typical of the acquiescence on the part of many church leaders: "I did listen respectfully to some very earnest young people and their views which differ from mine. I feel it is time that all ministers *listen* as well as *preach*. Truth does not begin and end with us."

In some instances youth may have much to tell the church that will help to reach their peers. But too many churches have abdicated their role of leadership and are desperately attempting to stem the exodus of youth through permissiveness and the aping of secular music styles. I am thankful for those churches that will continue to guide and educate youth and not the reverse. We face often an arrogant and conceited generation with meager spiritual knowledge and experience and yet some are convinced that their ideas are correct and their desires paramount. They need both our scriptural condemnation and our help.

Let us not give them what they want but rather what they need in church music—theologically supportable lyrics and melodies and rhythms that culturally elevate and spiritually bless. Let us summon them to worship, not to wiggle! In our desperate plight to reach young people, let us not emulate the mistake of Christian rock by catering to the whims of youth. Just because young people may not always want what we're giving them is no reason to give them what they want.

chapter six

BY THEIR
FRUITS

Many variables determine the effectiveness of an evangelistic outreach. This is especially the case with respect to Christian rock since the dedication of those using this approach varies considerably from group to group. There are some differences in tactics but the results of most Christian rock evangelistic endeavors are usually superficial.

Such an approach has attracted many participants who are enamoured with its youth appeal yet who lack a fundamental theological commitment. Their definition of spiritual success falls far short of historic evangelical standards.

By reason of the medium (rock) and the accompanying theological philosophy, the products of Christian rock should be judged on the following considerations.

Christian rock advocates are often sincere and do communicate with some who appear to make decisions for Christ but the ends do not justify the means.

Christian rock and its followers are usually sincere in their zeal to reach the souls of men and lead them to Christ. They observe the decline in church attendance and lagging interest on the part of youth that plagues many sectors of evangelical Christianity. They know, as all concerned Christians do, that the church will grow only if a massive spiritual awakening grips this generation.

Since the lives of millions of teenagers revolve around rock music, some leaders suggest that a Christian application of this style of music is an excellent point of contact. They point out that their approach usually gets a crowd and that there are usually many decisions for Christ on the records afterward. On this basis they reason that anti-rock arguments are merely academic and that their results speak for themselves.

By asking to be judged on the basis of results, Christian rock promoters operate on the principle of expediency. Unfortunately, such actions may negate God's will. To suggest that the ends justify the means is to launch upon a philosophy without stable principles and ethics. It is a tenuous philosophy even in secular concerns but a dangerous one in sacred endeavors. And end only justifies the means when both are consistent in content and scriptural authority. The church should be free to change and adapt, but only within the framework of spiritual responsibility. If this is missing, the focus is on the goal and the means are undertaken without the benefit of scriptural guidance.

Sincerity is a good quality, but it can be a deceptive guide. A noble purpose alone is not sufficient reason to justify tactics or to consider them beyond question. The error of the "new morality" is its dependence upon the supposedly sincere individual's unselfish love and concern for others. Christian rock mistakenly supposes that the means (rock music) should not be questioned if the motivation (evangelistic concern) is sincere. In fact, sincerity is often a mask to conceal the desire for money. When applied to church work, this is a serious charge. But the fact remains that those who have the most to gain from the church's adoption of rock music are composers, publishers and record companies who are eager to serve this vast consumer market. They have based a large portion of their production on the gamble that the evangelical church will accept their offerings. If it doesn't, a sizeable investment in publicity and printing will be lost.

This financial windfall is a valid reason for questioning the sincerity of the promoters of Christian rock. Composers, publishers and record companies know that the more they can get the church to act and sound like the world, the broader will be the base of their appeal. This is enough to lead one to the conclusion that sincerity should not be considered at all as a factor in judging the success of Christian rock.

We have made sacred cows out of the words "relate" and "communicate." Some people have assumed that achieving these ends must be the major goal of church music among youth. Logically, secular music forms provide a pre-conditioned medium with which to accomplish these ends. Since most church musicians are unfamiliar with such idioms, they seek the advice of musical personalities who live on both sides of the fence, drawing their musical income from the world while appeasing their consciences by partially catering to religious audiences.

The lives of such musicians are sometimes below even the moral par of unregenerates. In fact, their reputations represent precisely the opposite of what they profess to accomplish with church music. Because of their musical ability they are expected to know how to reach the world for which they work while professing not to be a part of it. This situation is ludicrous! Spiritual shipwrecks are setting the sails of church music.

It's hard to be honest and to evaluate objectively the ends of Christian rock. For one thing, it is too soon to tell what the full effects will be. The phenomenon of Christian rock has been around only since approximately 1968. There is still some question whether or not decisions in Christian rock concerts lead to genuine rebirth. Usually there is no clear-cut invitation to repentance at such affairs. If the explanation of steps to salvation is blurred, how can the way be found?

Some have speculated that more often than not, conversion to Christ at Christian rock concerts and musicals is not really a born-again experience but an identification with the person of Jesus within the perspective of the "groovy Christian life." Even those who have no anti-rock objections should wait until the fruit of its work can be evaluated. Christian rock is still in its unproven infancy. No one yet can objectively call the approach a success. And before the phenomenon can be properly evaluated the criterion must be first determined.

The tide of opinion is currently running in favor of Christian rock, but one encouraging fact should be noted. It has been my privilege to speak in many of the largest fundamental churches of America. These churches, which outspokenly endorse my anti-rock position, are among the fastest growing churches in the country. Their stand, taken on the basis of a strictly fundamental position, has been rewarded by strong, growing congregations. Their evangelistic ministries are producing solid, church-attending converts. Their church programs are going forward vigorously.

Those who say they are concerned about reaching souls by the multitudes through mass evangelism should examine the program of these churches. They are doing the job. Christian rock enthusiasts might be surprised to learn that their argument that the end justifies the means would have them coming up with far less success than the large fundamental churches are enjoying—churches which take a stand against the uncertain sound of Christian rock.

Christian rock promoters approve of the medium, therefore those who are won to Christ through it will remain with rock.

Rock is associated today with political radicalism, hippie life-styles, and the drug culture. In chapter five I established the fact that even the unsaved often link rock with sex. Christian rock promoters insist, however, that they use the idiom without any involvement in the associated evils. They argue that rock is considered immoral only because of the people who perform it. Rock performed by the right people under proper circumstances, they say, could be a force for good. They profess to take a stand against any anti-Christian elements in secular rock.

But rock is more than a musical form. It cannot be disassociated from its immoral trappings. It is a social phenomenon that has contributed to the growing evils of our permissive society caught in the grip of a socio-sexual revolution. To use rock is indeed to identify with the negative frustrations and philosophies of rock lovers rather than offering the positive assurance of hope in Christ.

79

The clear teaching of I Thessalonians 5:22 is that Christians are to "abstain from all appearance of evil." It is difficult to see how any involvement with rock would not violate such a standard. Those who are evangelized by Christian rock will have no reason to reject rock in its secular form. Converts will obviously continue to listen to rock. The rock they return to will not be softened by the spiritual perspective.

If Christian teenagers were to be given a choice between Christian rock and secular rock they would chose secular rock. Since rock may have contributed to the sinful condition of the new convert before his conversion it is doubtful that he could continue to grow in grace. The beat of rock music contributes nothing toward attaining spiritual maturity.

Lovers of Christian rock are forced to approve of secular rock. In fact, they often use it in their concerts and feed on a heavy diet of it themselves. How can they expect people who come to the Lord under their out-reach to do less? When the unsaved are reached with rock the blind are leading the blind. The unsuspecting convert thus becomes mired in the same quicksand that has kept his spiritual mentors from achieving full spiritual maturity.

I've had the privilege of counseling many seekers after Christ who were formerly on the rock scene. It has been necessary to make clear to them that they must adopt an anti-rock position at the start of their Christian life. Failure to do so will leave them open to satan's darts. It will allow him a foothold and block the channel of communication between them and their Lord.

Conversion is more than walking forward in a meeting and grasping the hand of the preacher. It's more than reciting a Bible verse or two. It's more than simply repeating a prayer. Christianity is a totally new way of life. The believer is walking on a new road. To be happy he must abandon those weights which kept him shackled. He plays under a new set of rules. But the joy of the Christian life can be easily marred if the convert keeps looking longingly back to the old ways.

Those who embark on their walk with Christ are not likely to enjoy it to the fullest if their lives are filled with the jarring beat of rock music. The spiritual fruit of Christian rock evangelism is usually a shallow experience held by one who has "turned on" with Christ rather than one who has taken up the cross and entered into the discipline of discipleship.

chapter seven

SHEDDING

THE

MYTHS

Young people are gradually taking the lead in population statistics. In significant ways they are influencing the future policies of all segments of society, including the church. Most evangelical churches in recent years have not found a program to minister effectively to youth. The spiritual drop-out rate remains high. Fewer young men and women than ever are candidates for full-time Christian service.

Is the church entirely to blame? The Bible clearly predicts a falling away in the last days. Certainly the hedonistic, godless age in which we live fits with increasing exactness the picture of apostasy revealed in the Scriptures.

The church cannot blame all its problems on the world, of course. It must constantly undergo critical self-analysis so it can adopt more effective techniques in its ministry in Christ's name to a lost and dying world.

83

At the start, we must rid our thinking of several myths. Some would have us to believe that this age and generation require unique evangelistic techniques. But this is not necessarily so. Despite the uniqueness of this generation of young people they do not respond more readily to bizarre innovative approaches than to tried and tested methods of simple gospel preaching. The basic human problems which find their solutions in the Gospel have not changed. The Gospel has not changed either. Our commission to preach it has not changed. Therefore we are commanded not to major on techniques but to *preach*! When people come to Christ it is because of a quest for reality prompted by the conviction of the Holy Spirit, not because they suddenly find themselves turned on with some mystic vibrations. If they respond because of a Christian rock publicity campaign designed to present the Christian life as superior in temporal benefits, their Christian experience may be shallow and unproductive.

Another myth that must be laid to rest is the idea that a "turned off" audience requires the speaker to "turn off" his message, or at least to colloquialize it almost beyond recognition. The Apostles were never convinced that failure to produce results and outright opposition meant any change whatever in their message. They simply shook the dust off their feet and continued on their way until they found those who were desperate for reality and interested enough to listen.

The most disastrous myth of all, and one used to bolster the use of Christian rock, is the supposition that large crowds and many "decisions" spell spiritual success. Christ warned His disciples not to expect phenomenal success. He told them, "If they have persecuted me they will also persecute you" (John 15:20). The early disciples never considered tailoring the Gospel in order to accomodate the particular philosophies of their audience.

Jesus plainly stated that those who found the narrow way would be few. Paul's sermons did not always draw large audiences. Some even criticized his personal speaking appearance and doubtless suggested that his lack of obvious success in the confrontation with the Athenian philosophers was due to an approach that was too rigid and negative.

When the church sheds these myths it will be in a good position to address a sin-crippled generation of youth. Peter and John might well say to our generation: "Expensive musical extravaganzas, choreographic dance routines, hip life styles and rock rhythms have we none. But such as we have give we unto you. In the name of Jesus, rise up and walk!"

Three factors should be considered in determining the role of music evangelism to present Christ.

1. The lyrical text should be considered first. Some experimentation with church music idioms actually alters the message. When the nature of sin is soft-peddled and Christ's blood atonement on the cross obscured, the lyrics are unworthy of the Gospel.

I fear that too much contemporary gospel music has been lyrically subjective, focusing on the human dilemma to the exclusion of the divine solution. We must return to objective statements of scriptural truth —a characteristic of great church music that has endured. Gospel music does certainly have a place, but the historic songs of the Church must not be tossed out and considered irrelevant. Both may be effective witnesses under the appropriate circumstances and in the right environment.

No two contemporary gospel songs are alike. Each must be individually considered for its own merit. But the ultimate theme of every song must be Christ. Directly or indirectly, the lyrical focus must be a positive proclamation of hope in Him, not just a wistful longing after Someone in the sky.

2. The most elusive aspect of contemporary music is its beat, yet that too must be laid on the block and analyzed. In these hectic days, secular music often reflects our fast-paced life style. Yet Christ offers peace and serenity even in times like these.

Church music ought to reflect this antithesis. Christian rock does not. It prefers instead to use the savage beat of rock. There are, however, varying degrees in the "hardness" of the rock beat that is used in church. The spectrum runs from acid Christian rock to a middle-of-the-road pop style. However, both have a definite, pulsating or syncopated beat.

Where can we draw the line? That remains a problem particularly with those who have little musical experience. The author's book *Rock & Roll: The Devil's Diversion* will provide useful guidelines in this dilemma.

Personal tastes of listeners further compound the problem. Some Christians, because of their cultural background, prefer simplistic melodies with lively rhythms while others may prefer anthems and hymns. Those in the latter category sometimes criticize youth-oriented music purely out of personal distaste rather than because of any spiritual perception. This is unfortunate because they may be correct in their criticism but unjust in their reasoning.

The person who criticizes should do so because of valid, objective reasoning, not just out of personal tastes. I believe that ultimately the Holy Spirit can lead sincere Christians to make the correct decisions in these matters. Certainly any use of a pulsating or syncopated beat should be open to question. Extreme accentuation of such rhythms should definitely be rejected.

3. The manner and environment of each presentation should be considered. Informal forms of religious music such as a pure folk idiom may be accept-

able at a youth gathering. But the same musical diet would be unsuited to a Sunday morning worship or communion service. Southern-style gospel music can be presented in an unobjectionable way with God's blessing. But an uncommitted group can turn the same song into a frivolous, spiritually superficial rendition that dishonors God.

The time is long overdue for the church to take a stand against novices whose lives are not compatible with the exhortations of their singing. This criterion would eliminate many Christian rock groups.

The lack of a firm hand by spiritual leaders has allowed many groups to sing tunes right on the church platform that would be more appropriately performed in a rock concert hall. Dance routines and hip-swinging sensous numbers cannot have the touch of God's Spirit even when the message of the song is scriptural. A talent dedicated to God with a tastefully presented song will accomplish what lavish costuming, highly polished professionalism and showmanship cannot.

I am not suggesting that Christian musicals should be second rate. God deserves our best efforts, but also our prayerfully, conscientious efforts as well.

This book concerns itself with the importance of church music. But perhaps an over-emphasis on the role of music in presenting the Gospel is part of our problem. The lives of youth revolve around music. Many have naturally concluded, therefore, that music ought to be the major thrust in youth evangelism. Could it be that the evangelical church has forgotten the priority of a *preached* gospel?

Romans 10:13 declares: "For whosoever shall call upon the name of the Lord shall be saved. How then shall they call on Him in whom they have not believed? and how shall they believe in Him of whom they have not heard? and how shall they hear without a preacher?"

The Gospel is not to be debated or compared or analyzed. It is to be proclaimed with warning, denunciation, and hope in Christ—all by preaching.

No great religious movement has ever derived its initial momentul from music. The role of music has always been an accompaniment to preaching. Even some Christian rock promoters admit that the results they manage to obtain are usually more attributable to the personal testimonies and sermonettes interwoven into their program format than to the Christian rock songs themselves.

In the days of the Reformation five centuries ago it was not uncommon for crowds to listen to sermons two and three hours long. Today young people will spend two and three *days* at a rock fest, enduring all sorts of privations just for the sake of music. Do advocates of Christian rock really believe that they compel allegiance to the Gospel by giving young people more of what they already crave?

A careful study of God's Word reveals only one method of evangelism—the preaching of the Scripture. If the Apostle Paul were advising a young person today I'm sure he would exhort him as he did Timothy long ago: "Preach the Word" (II Timothy 4:2). For an innovative generation proud of its cynicism, such advice may seem too closely aligned with the "Establishment." But our Lord was a preacher. He chose to conceive the church at Pentecost by winning its first converts by preaching.

Rock is the pivot upon which crucial decisions of the evangelical church ministry will turn. The question remains: Will this generation be evangelized by the gospel of rock or by the preaching of repentance, of redemption, of regeneration—the Gospel of Jesus Christ, the Son of God?

FOOTNOTES

Chapter Two

1. *Hit Parader,* Feb. 1971, p. 10.
2. *Time,* June 22, 1970, p. 59.
3. *Rolling Stone,* Sept. 16, 1970, p. 48.
4. *Billboard,* Nov. 7, 1970, p. 1.
5. *Hit Parader,* March 1969, p. 18.
6. *Billboard,* Nov. 7, 1970, p. 1.
7. *Rolling Stone,* May 28, 1970, p. 9.
8. *Rolling Stone,* May 14, 1970, p. 20.
9. *Hit Parader,* Jan. 1971, p. 27.
10. *Time,* Nov. 9, 1970, p. 47.
11. *Time,* Nov. 9, 1970, p. 47.
12. *Rolling Stone,* April 16, 1970, p. 48.
13. *Rolling Stone,* April 16, 1970, p. 48.
14. *Teen,* July 1970, p. 80.

Chapter Three

1, *News in the World of Religion,* July 7, 1970.
2. *Christian Life,* Nov., 1970, p. 24.
3. *Christian Life,* June, 1970, p. 21.
4. *Christianity Today,* Sept. 25, 1970, p. 25.
5. *Christian Life,* Oct., 1970, p. 14.
6. *Billboard,* Oct. 10, 1970, p. 56.
7. *Decision,* Oct. 1969, p. 3.
8. *Newsweek,* May 11, 1970, p. 77.
9. *Christianity Today,* March 27, 1970, p. 36.

Chapter Four

1. *Newsweek,* Sept. 5, 1966, p. 80.
2. *Billboard,* Oct. 18, 1969, p. 12.
3. *Rolling Stone,* April 2, 1970, p. 12.

Chapter Five

1. *Time,* April 13, 1970, p. 103.
2. *Seventeen,* April 1970, p. 98.
3. *Life,* June 28, 1968, p. 83.
4. *Hit Parader,* March 1969, p. 18.
5. *Do It,* Simon & Schuster, N.Y., N.Y., pp. 18-19.
6. *Pageant,* "Age of Go-Go," pp. 127-128.
7. *Encyclopedia Britannica,* Vol. 7, 1965, p. 39.
8. Jude 9, Bible.
9. *Hit Parader,* Nov. 1968, p. 38.
10. *Time,* April 13, 1970, p. 103.
11. *Hit Parader,* Jan. 1970, p. 15.